INDELIBLE EVIDENCE

BLITZ EDITIONS

LAB DETECTION
Scientific Evidence

From Henry Faulds' original pioneering ideas on fingerprinting to the ultra-modern process of DNA testing was a quantum leap that was accomplished in little more than a century. It is a leap that has spelled nothing but bad news for society's villains, now unable to rely on a good alibi.

No-one on earth laments the passing of the "good old days" more than the professional criminal. For as time has gone by, so the arm of the law has grown ever longer thanks to the miracles of forensic science. Applying chemistry, physics, biology and pathology to sleuthing has combined to give us space-age methods of divining criminal acts and, thereby, bringing the perpetrators of them to justice. Just as the safebreaker in early-Victorian times would scoff at the very idea that a single fingerprint could lead him to swing from the gallows, so the murderer of the 1970s didn't realise that within a decade a single drop of blood would give sleuths his very genetic make-up in the process now known as DNA.

Before science was applied to crime the catching of society's miscreants was pretty much a hit-and-miss affair. Unless a murder weapon or stolen property was found upon the culprit – or he was marked by the signs of struggle with his victim – there was every likelihood that he would get clean away with his misdeed. One of the earliest and most significant crime-fighting techniques to be taken on board by police authorities all over the world must, of course, be the process of fingerprinting. In 1864 in India a servant of Her Majesty's empire named William Herschel noted that no two fingerprints are ever alike and began using the system to pay pensioned Indian Army soldiers who could not read and write; the presence of their right index finger print each payday testified to their identity. His system was improved upon some years later by a dour Scotsman named Henry Faulds, who in 1880 wrote to Nature magazine suggesting that this might be a way of identifying "society's criminal elements". There followed a certain amount of acrimonious squabbling between the two gentlemen as to who had rights to the aforementioned "discovery" but, nonetheless, between them they had discovered the system of logging criminals that is still in place today.

It was a third individual, Sir Francis Galton, who took the "dab" out of the realms of the possible into the practical. In 1892 he published a book called simply *Fingerprints* which proved conclusively that no two were ever alike. That same year the first murder ever to be solved by fingerprinting was committed in Necochea, Argentina. A woman named Francesca Rojas ran into the hut of her neighbour screaming that her two children aged four and six had been murdered. She put the blame on a man named Velasquez who she said had been pressuring her to marry, saying that she had returned home from work and found the children dead in bed. Velasquez was tortured by the local police but he maintained his innocence. Colin Wilson, Author of *The Mammoth Book of True Crime*, takes up the story: "A police

Below: *A celebrated case in which 'dabs' found at the crime scene proved the undoing of kidnap-killer Arthur Hosein.*

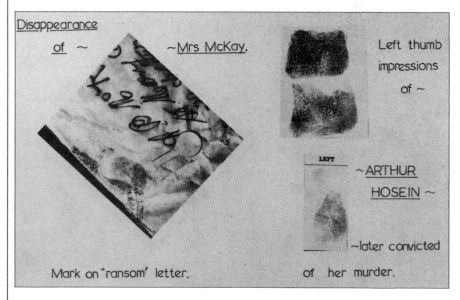

Disappearance of ~ ~Mrs McKay. Mark on "ransom" letter. Left thumb impressions of ~ LEFT ~ARTHUR HOSEIN ~ ~later convicted of her murder.

Opposite: *Henry Faulds, founding father of modern detection.*

Above: *Dusting a bottle for fingerprints – the film left behind clearly shows the imprint.*

broke down and confessed – she had murdered her two children because she wanted to marry a young lover who objected to them. This Argentine Lady Macbeth, who tried to rid herself of illegitimate children and an unwanted lover with one blow, obviously deserves to stand very high on a list of the world's worst women."

Nowadays the FBI in America is the repository of the most fingerprints on earth, over 200 million of them that can all be accessed by the major law enforcement agencies in the country within minutes. The FBI handles 30,000 fingerprint enquiries each day using laser beams to scan 80 fingerprints a second to find a match. In Britain there are some two-and-a-half million fingerprints on file on the police national computer in Hendon.

SOPHISTICATED DETECTION

While the collating and keeping of fingerprints has grown more technical, so has their retrieval from crime scenes. Iodine fumes and niohydrin spray can be used to lift prints from porous surfaces. Even lip-prints can be classified and there is a case of a hit-and-run driver in America where the lip-prints of the victim were taken from the bumper of the suspect's vehicle. But only two per-cent of crimes are solved by fingerprints today, even though their importance cannot be underestimated.

A single print was enough to trap John Cannan in Britain in 1987 for the abduction and sex murder of newlywed Shirley Banks. Cannan, 25, was caught driving the woman's car but claimed to have purchased it at an auction. He insisted he had never met the woman – she was missing, presumed dead – and police were still on the hunt for clues. A police search of his flat in Bristol turned up a dossier from a private detective Cannan had hired – and on it was a single fingerprint. This was matched from prints that were taken from the dead woman's home and office. Paul Jobbins, a senior fingerprint officer with Avon police, was gratified to see his work lead to Cannan being sentenced to life imprisonment for murder and rape.

After the evolution of fingerprinting came blood as the next weapon in the arsenal of law and order. Its unique properties, which enabled scientists to develop serums

inspector named Alvarez went out to investigate from La Plata. And he knew something about the work of a Dalmatian named Juan Vucetich, head of the Statistical Bureau of Police in Buenos Aires who had developed his own fingerprint system after reading an article by Galton. Alvarez went into the woman's hut and searched for clues. All he could find was a bloody thumb-print on a door. Alvarez sawed off the portion of the door and took it back to headquarters. Then he sent for Rojas and made her give a thumb-print. Alvarez knew very little about classification, but it was quite obvious that the two prints were identical. When he showed the woman the two prints through a magnifying glass, she against diptheria and snake bites, could be used to identify the perpetrators of crime using simple laboratory tests. Initially the process merely told investigators whether blood was human or animal – as in the case of a French murderer who was sent to the guillotine in 1902 after a test showed that the blood he was covered with was not from a rabbit as claimed but from a human being – and soon blood was classified into three separate groupings thanks to the research of the Austrian-born scientist Dr. Karl Landsteiner. Landsteiner, who emigrated to America, received the Nobel prize in 1930 for his work in classifying blood – a boon to doctors, hospitals and patients, but no less a landmark discovery for sleuths. His OAB system categorised humans as having type O, type A or type B blood groups, all classified according to their immunological properties.

Twenty years before this, in 1910 in England, came the first British murder trial at which blood was to play a crucial role. Isabella Wilson, a 70-year-old junkshop keeper, was found brutalised and strangled to death in the back of her premises in Slough. A shifty character named William Broome, who had designs upon acquiring the shabby store, was a chief suspect in the murder but had moved away on the day she was found dead. Police later tracked him down to Harlesden in North London where a prostitute friend gave him an alibi that he had been with her when the old lady was being killed. But Dr. William Wilcox, the chief expert on bloodstains at the Home Office, found traces of blood under the victim's fingernails – traces which he matched to scratches on Broome's face. Broome probably did not derive any satisfaction from the fact that, as he mounted the gallows to be hanged for the murder, he had gone into the criminal history books as the first villain to be brought to book by blood.

MISSING EVIDENCE

Another famous murder case was once solved because of the *lack* of bloodstains. A famous French criminologist named Alexandre Lacassagne plotted the correlation between blood spots at a crime scene and the position of the victim at the time of death. For instance: blood dropped vertically from a stationary object makes a circular spot with ragged edges. The greater the distance the blood has to drop, the greater the crenellations. If blood moves from a moving object it leaves spots resembling exclamation marks indicating the direction the victim was heading in. Thanks to Professor Lacassagne, police forces were able to draw up charts for crime scene detectives to reconstruct what had happened to murder victims.

Such a chart came in useful for the examination of 43-year-old Catherine McCluskey, found lying in the middle of the road in Glasgow on July 29 1950. At first appearances the corpse seemed to have been dragged along the road by a car or lorry, a long trail of blood marking her path along the tarmac.

Professor Andrew Alison, the pathologist working on the case, examined the body and he concluded that her injuries were not consistent with having been knocked down by a hit-and-run driver. He surmised that she had either been bludgeoned and dragged to make it look like an accident or that she had been deliberately run over – murdered. The victim was a woman with numerous boyfriends, all of

Below: *In 1864 in India, a servant of Her Majesty's empire, William Herschel, noted that no two fingerprints were ever alike and began using the system to pay off pensioned Indian Army soldiers.*

considerable amounts of blood on his trousers if he had indeed tried to free her. There was not a speck. So, too, another killer went to the gallows because of blood – this time because of the lack of it.

As the ways to kill a human being became more sophisticated it became necessary for police forces to equip themselves with the technology to catch murderers. The greatest challenges for lab experts have come from firearms, where the study known as ballistics has become an art unto itself. It was in Paris in May 1912, at the Congress of Legal Medicine, that ballistics was accepted as a new branch of forensic science in its own right.

The necessity for this had been the advancements in firearms, particularly cheap ones like those made by Colt in America, which took guns out of the hands of the ruling class and put them into the grip of a great mass of seething, discontented people – the proletariat. Ballistics works in much the same way as fingerprinting. Every gun has a unique signature which leaves its mark upon bullets fired into a victim. Tracing the gun is usually the first step in solving the crime.

At the Paris conference in 1912 Professor Victor Balthazard, an eminent expert, spoke of a case in which a man named Guillotin had been shot dead. Upon

whom were tracked down by police. One of them even turned out to be a policeman, James Robertson, who soon became the main suspect in her death. His home was searched and a large quantity of stolen property was found. Although an indication of his dishonesty, it didn't pin a deliberate murder on him.

But he broke under questioning and said that he accidentally knocked her over after dropping her off at home and that he moved the car "backwards and forwards in an attempt to free her". When this failed, he claimed, he at first tried to pull the woman free but then panicked and left the body there.

This "confession" was unmasked as the fallacy it was by the fact that the victim had no injuries to her legs. Professor John Glaister, an expert in Lacassagne's methods, had said that there would have been

examination, his body was found to contain several bullets. When the main suspect in the case, a man called Houssard, was brought into custody, Professor Balthazard was brought in to examine his weapon. Local firearms experts in the south of France were unable to detect whether or not the bullets had been fired from his gun, but Balthazard was able to point out no less than 86 similarities between his gun barrel and marks on the bullets. Houssard was guillotined and Balthazard's methods of comparing marks on projectiles to the metal tubes that expelled them laid the foundations for ballistic science.

A member of the New York State prosecutor's office called Charles Waite refined that science into the art it has become. He devoted his life to firearms investigation, spurred on by a trial in America in which a man's life was spared because of proof that a bullet which killed a man had come from a gun other than his own. For ten years, with the aid of gun manufacturers across

Above: *The crime at Katyn Wood. Forensic evidence showed that the mass slaughter was by Stalin's killers.*

Opposite Top: *James Robertson – a lack of bloodstains at the scene of Catherine McCluskey's demise pinned her murder on him.*

Opposite Below: *The body of his victim, which he had despatched by running over her in a car.*

America, he catalogued every type of weapon together with the signature that it left upon bullets. Next he began chronicling European imports and then, to refine the system even further, approached the Bausch and Lomb Optical Company to make him a microscope for comparing bullets. A man named Philip Gravelle then proceeded to invent the "comparison microscope" which could place a test bullet next to a murder scene bullet for instant comparison. A physicist called John H. Fischer then made a device called a helixometer, a slender, lighted probe for the study of gun barrels. Armed, as it were, with all this new information, Waite and Calvin Goddard, a friend and former army doctor, set up the Bureau of Forensic Ballistics in New York in 1923.

Ballistic knowledge was vigorously pursued all over the world. The greatest mass-exhumation of bodies for forensic study of the bullets that put them in the ground was carried out by Nazi Germany.

Above: *Dr Hawley Harvey Crippen. Poisons found in the stomach of his wife caught the sinsister but clever physician.*

GENERALS AND
LIEUTENANTS WERE BOUND
AND SHOT IN THE BACK OF
THE HEAD AND BURIED IN
MASSIVE LIME PITS

In 1940, some 4,000 Polish officers, from generals to lieutenants, were bound and shot in the back of the head and buried in massive lime pits shrouded by the towering fir trees that made up the forest of Katyn, near Smolensk in Western Russia. The corpses were discovered during Germany's invasion of Russia in 1943 and immediate propaganda was made of it – the Germans said that they had been murdered by the NKVD, Stalin's dreaded butchers. All the victims had their hands tied to a macabre noose around their necks which tightened if they struggled, all bore the same single-entry head wound testifying to their methodical execution.

It was later learned the liquidations at the Katyn Forest began on April 3 1941 and did not end until May 13, five weeks later. In the previous week the prisoners were rounded up in their respective camps at Kozelsk, Starobelsk and Ostashkov and taken in batches of 50 to 500 to railheads to board cattlewagons for unknown destinations. It was the 4,400 prisoners of the Kozelsk camp whose final halt was to be the forest at Katyn.

Dr. Gerhard Buhtz, a professor of forensic medicine from a leading German university, was put in charge of the exhumation and examination of the grave pits which were re-opened in early March 1943. For ten weeks the stink of rotten flesh and Egyptian tobacco – the Germans smoked it to mask the smell of the dead – mingled with the scents of moss and pine sap as the murdered men were disinterred and laid out. Three separate commissions were invited by the Germans into Katyn. The first was entirely German, the second composed of scientists and forensic experts from Switzerland, Belgium, Hungary and Bulgaria and the third entirely Polish. The evidence was mightily in favour of the German viewpoint. Although the ammunition was German, records from the manufacturing plants showed it to be batches sold to Lithuania before the war which was later seized by NKVD police units. Buhtz used the tests pioneered by Waite to test the bullets and the guns from which they came – there was no doubt that the Soviets were to blame for the massacre.

THE APPLIANCE OF SCIENCE

For close to five decades the crime at Katyn Wood remained the single biggest whodunnit of World War Two. The Germans claimed that the Russians had done it, the Russians that the Germans were the perpetrators. But simple scientific facts proved that it was a Soviet crime. Stalin was able to do many things as dictator, but altering indisputable scientific facts was not one of them.

It is far from Europe and Russia, in America, where the need for ballistic science remains greatest. Among the population there are 75 million guns – and rising. Sixty three people die each day from firearms while in Britain and other European countries, firearms deaths are still minimal. Each day the FBI ballistics unit increases its knowledge to take on board details of the latest killing weapons, like machine guns and pump-action shotguns being used by the drug gangs and the mobsters. When it comes to ballistics, the Americans lead the world.

But it is probably fair to say that when it comes to stone cold corpses, Britain must take much credit for criminal pathology. In this century great criminal pathologists like Bernard Spilsbury, Francis Camps and Keith Simpson have helped to solve some of the most baffling murder cases. British medicine has always enjoyed an enviable reputation around the globe – it followed that the application of that to crime detection produced some of the most brilliant medico-legal brains of all time. What do they look for when first presented with that mass of cold flesh that was once a living, breathing human being? And how can they tell what the cause of death was when often all they are presented with is a pile of decomposing or burned flesh wrapped around a few skeletal bones?

SUREFIRE CLUES

Of course, that is their trade and what may seem the medical equivalent of looking for a needle in a haystack is often elementary. No smoke on lung tissue on a charred corpse means death before the fire – there was no inhalation. Similarly, no water in the lungs of a "drowning" victim means they were dead before they hit the water. Broken bones in the throat of a corpse found by an empty bottle of pills means the tablets were forced down instead of being swallowed voluntarily.

And what layman could have found in over 400lbs of human "sludge" – rendered down by the acid of notorious killer John George Haigh – a single gallstone and single hairpin? Professor Keith Simpson found them and they were the clues which sent Haigh to the gallows as one of the most notorious killers in British history.

Identifying a corpse from just a few particles of flesh and bone is, of course, the hardest task facing forensic pathologists, but it is one which they invariably rise to the occasion to meet. Sir Bernard Spilsbury, who became as famous as a pop star might be nowadays because of his awesome presence in court and unmatched knowledge of crime, cut his teeth on some of the most infamous murders in British

history – including one that bears the name of a man known from the jungles of the Amazon to the ice floes of the Arctic: Dr. Crippen. Sir Bernard was 33 and unknighted when he became involved in the Crippen case in 1910, but his success in that most chilling of cases only served to propel him into forensic fame.

Dr. Hawley Crippen was an American-born physician working in London whose attentions wandered from his wife Belle – dominant, overbearing, cool towards the bespectacled doctor – towards a mistress called Ethel Neave, who took the fancy name Ethel LeNeve because she thought it made her more sophisticated. Although he divorced his wife she hovered on the periphery of Crippen's life with Ethel, casting a long shadow over his new, younger lover. He decided that shadow could only be lifted with her death, which he duly

WHEN IT COMES TO STONE COLD CORPSES, BRITAIN MUST TAKE MUCH CREDIT FOR CRIMINAL PATHOLOGY

Below: *Ethel LeNeve, mistress of the wicked Dr Crippen.*

dispensed by poisoning her, dismembering her and covering what remained of the corpse with quicklime and fleeing to America to begin life afresh in the New World. Chief Inspector Walter Drew of Scotland Yard sent the famous telegraphic warning that served as the first Marconi message to arrest a murderer.

It was left to Spilsbury to examine what was left to determine what had killed her and if her death could be pinned on Crippen. Firstly, Spilsbury was able to prove the traces of hyoscine poison in her stomach – a poison which the good doctor had purchased shortly before she vanished. Brian Marriner, the respected author of *On Death's Bloody Trail*, a work on forensic science, wrote: "Then the next most important clue was a piece of flesh from the abdomen which bore an operation scar – as had Mrs. Crippen. Defence experts claimed it was just a piece of flesh from the thigh, and the scar was just a fold in the skin. Spilsbury, in his calm and patient manner, showed that it came from the abdomen, pointing out that part of the rectus muscle of the abdominal wall was still attached to the specimen in question. He had shamed his elders with superior knowledge." Spilsbury won that case and many hundreds more before his own loneliness and demons drove him to take his own life.

SILENT TESTIMONY

Forensic pathologists are also invaluable for those crimes to which there have been no witnesses. When Juliet Marion Hulme and Pauline Yvonne Parker were brought before the Crown in Christchurch, New Zealand, in 1954, the case received worldwide attention because of its morbid themes. Like the case of the Chicago thrill killers Loeb and Leopold – a couple of intellectuals who killed a small boy in the mistaken belief that they could get away with the perfect murder – psychologists were at pains to try to explain the fusion of two normal, caring minds into a single unit bent on misery and death. For that is what Juliet and Pauline descended to when they feared that their parents were bent on breaking up their friendship.

In a bid to forestall or prevent the break-up they believed was coming they plotted, and carried out, the murder of Mrs. Honora

Mary Parker. Mrs. Parker, 45, Pauline's mother, was bludgeoned repeatedly to death by the vile duo who tried to cover their tracks by claiming she had fallen. It was on June 22 1954 that two hysterical girls, covered in blood, shattered the tranquility of the afternoon tea ritual at a sedate Christchurch restaurant when they burst through the doors. "Mummy's been hurt," blurted out Pauline. "She's hurt, covered with blood." Tearfully they begged the manageress of the restaurant to phone for police while they gulped down sugared tea in an apparent attempt to ease their shock.

Below: *The wicked duo Juliet Marion Hulme and Pauline Parker after their arrest for the murder of Pauline's mother.*

Some of the customers went with the police and the girls to a beauty spot in a nearby park that was close to a small bridge over a stream. Lying in a pool of blood, with her face unrecognisable, was Mrs. Parker. She was quite dead.

There were no witnesses to what had happened and immediate sympathy was with the hysterical girls. They explained she had fallen on a rocky path and that she had banged her head and died.

It wasn't until the pathologist examined the corpse and said there was bruising around the throat consistent with her having been held down as blow after blow – he speculated as many as 49   was rained down on her head. The girls were sent away for long periods.

POISONOUS INDIVIDUALS

Another speciality of the forensic boffins is venom. Poison has always been a form of murder that British killers have been partic ularly fond of. One of them, Graham Young, was of that breed who thought himself cleverer than the experts pitted against him. But he too would go down in the record books – not only for his victims, but because he was trapped due to the miracles of forensic science.

From his earliest days the boy who would grow up to become immortalised as The Broadmoor Poisoner was spellbound by potions which slowly squeezed the life out of his helpless victims. A thrill killer, it was the sensation of power which fuelled his manic desires and his intelligence which masked his wicked games.

When he was finally caught for poisoning his aunt, his father and his school chum – luckily they didn't die although he had at 14 murdered his stepmother and got away with it – he spent nine years in Broadmoor, only to be released from incarceration to murder twice more.

In April 1971, after he had been released, came the job advertisement in a local paper which would seal his fate – and that of several of his workmates. He saw an offer of employment with the John Hadland company of Bovingdon, in Hertfordshire, for a storeman's position. Hadland's was an old established family firm that manufactured high grade optical and photographic equipment.

Above: *One of the most famous pathologists Britain has ever produced – Professor Keith Simpson.*

> POISON HAS ALWAYS BEEN A FORM OF MURDER THAT BRITISH KILLERS HAVE BEEN PARTICULARLY FOND OF

He impressed managing director Godfrey Foster at his interview, and explained that his long time away from regular employment was due to a nervous breakdown he had suffered. Foster checked up with the training centre and also Broadmoor, but received such glowing references as to the young man's abilities and recovery that he offered him the job.

On Monday May 10 1971 Graham Young arrived at Hadlands. The company thought that they were getting a storeman. In reality they had hired an angel of death. With his £24-per-week wages he rented a £4-per-week bedsitter which in short order became his own little shop of horrors.

He lined his cupboards and shelves with an increasing collection of poisons, among them the antimony tartrate with which he had begun his fledgling career as a poisoner.

Above: *Computers like these are now used by Scotland Yard and major crimefighting agencies around the world to store information on criminals.*

THEY WERE BEING SLOWLY POISONED BY THALLIUM, A SEVERELY RESTRICTED POISON THAT IS USED TO KILL RATS

At work he was regarded, in turns, as a quiet, often distant young man or a belligerent, persistent speaker if he touched on the subjects of politics or chemistry. His best friend at work was 41-year-old Ron Hewitt, whose job he was taking. Ron stayed on to show the new man the ropes and introduced him to the other hands in the plant. Many showed great kindness to Young, lending him money and giving him cigarettes when he had none. Young repaid their affection and warmth by being the first one at the tea trolley when it trundled in during morning breaks.

The terror had begun.

On Thursday June 3, less than a month after he started there, Bob Egle, 59, who worked as storeroom boss, was taken ill with diarrhoea, cramps and nausea. Next, Ron Hewitt fell violently ill, suffering the same symptoms accompanied by acute stomach pains and burning sensations at the back of his throat. Workers at Hadlands called the mystery pains "the bug". In fact they were being slowly poisoned by thallium, a severely restricted poison used to kill rats that is so toxic it can cause death merely by being handled. Young bought the poison from chemists in London and was putting the tasteless, odourless chemical into his workmates' teas. On Wednesday July 7 Bob Egle died. His was a horrible, painful death, caused by a paralysis which spread throughout his body before it caused his heart to fail. There was no inquest on his body because doctors misinterpreted his illness as being bronchial-pneumonia linked to polyneuritis.

In September, after a relatively quiet summer, in which Young was often away, the nightmare continued. Fred Biggs, a part-time worker, was the next target. After 20 days of agonising cramps and pains he died. Four other workers were poisoned, two of them ending up in hospital with all their hair gone and with severe cases of depression brought on by the poison that they had ingested through the tainted tea.

It wasn't until Hadlands brought in a local doctor, Iain Anderson, to talk to staff and try to track down what was poisoning the workforce, that the noose began closing around Young's neck. Anderson said he had run down numerous checks but was unable to determine the source of the "bug". Young, unable to suppress his own ego over his knowledge of poisons, soon took the meeting over.

He reeled off mind-numbing statistics about poison and its effects – so much so that Anderson became suspicious. After consulting with the company management, Scotland Yard was called in. They ran a background check on all company employees – a move that was guaranteed to shine the light on the unsavoury past activities of Graham Young.

A COLD-HEARTED KILLER

Forensic scientists from the government research station at Aldermaston were called in and it was believed that thallium had caused the deaths and the illnesses. Thallium is a metal-based poison that has no smell, is colourless and tasteless. Young was arrested at his father's house, making himself an egg sandwich. As he was being led away he said to police: "Which ones are they doing me for, then?" The authorities were concerned that they did not have enough evidence on Young, and as both the bodies of his victims had been burned they feared he would, quite literally, get away with murder once again.

But in a forensic first the ashes of one of the cremated corpses showed traces of thallium in them. A process that is called "atomic absorption spectrometry" was deployed in which five micrograms of Thallium per gram of ash were found. On December 3 he was charged with murdering Egle. Now he wanted maximum publicity – the notoriety of Crippen and others that he now felt he had rightly earned. So he pleaded not guilty.

Later he was also charged with the murder of Fred Biggs and the attempted murders of two others and of further administering poison to two others. He went into the history books and captivity at St. Albans Court in 1972.

Now the world of the forensic expert is shifting away from blood and bone, hair and tissue, into the realm of sci-fi where lasers and electron microscopes are at the forefront of the war on crime.

The forensic science laboratory of Scotland Yard is now one of the most highly advanced criminal investigation labs on earth, where great emphasis and faith is being placed on laser technology. Graham Jackson, the Met's laser expert, likes to joke that he can literally make "clues glow in the dark" with his technology. He cites the case, for instance, of an Essex policeman who had been asked to look out for a truck involved in a hit-and-run case.

IN A FORENSIC FIRST THE ASHES OF ONE OF THE CREMATED CORPSES SHOWED TRACES OF THALLIUM

Below: *Graham Young, the Broadmoor poisoner, who sent so many innocents to their deaths.*

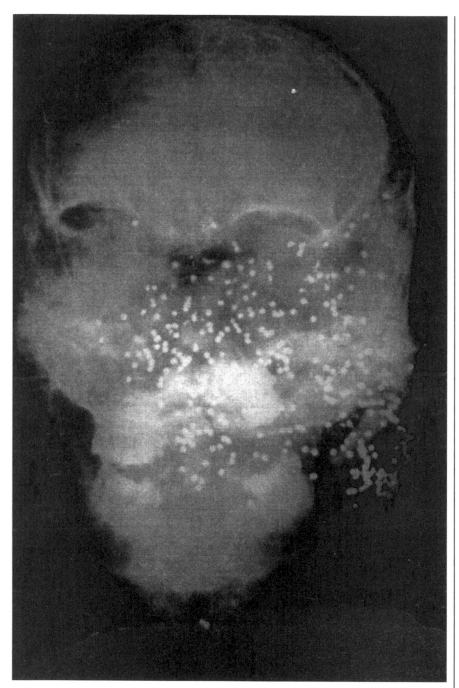

Above: *A head x-ray showing a pattern of shotgun pellets on the victim's left side.*

forensic lab. According to Dr. Ray Williams, the lab's director, the number showed up on his hand after it was subjected to laser-light! "He was not so much astonished by the technology but relieved that his hand was still in one piece," said Dr. Williams.

Laser technology is now also coming into its own in the field of fingerprinting. Until recently, the standard method of gleaning fingerprints from a crime scene was to dust aluminium powder over everything and hope that it stuck. For various reasons it may not – and in the old days that would have been the end of it.

But thanks to lasers many acids found in the ordinary human fingerprint fluoresce under laser light. In a darkened room the display can be spectacular – hundreds of "dabs" showing up where ordinary aluminium powder failed to detect them. The lights can also read underneath the correction fluid pasted over a word to reveal the word that was corrected.

Jackson said: "It has improved previous methods of detection considerably. Things like shoeprints, fingerprints, fibres, marks on bodies, stains and so on. It has proved possible to recover these types of evidence on occasions when often they cannot be seen at all by the human eye."

A METICULOUS MICROSCOPE

The scanning electron microscope is another high-tech tool worth its weight in gold. This uses electron beams instead of rays of light to identify fingerprints in circumstances which, on the surface, may seem impossible. For example, gunmen often carry firearms in rolled-up newspapers, the surface of which no-one believed a fingerprint could be retrieved from. A fingerprint on a picture, for example, is made up of thousands of tiny dots which would interfere with a laser scan. But the electron microscope can get around the problem. Firstly, the forensic scientist paints the page with a liquid containing a suspension of silver. When it comes into contact with the fingerprint the silver separates. When the page is then scanned the fingerprint stands out because the heavy silver atoms bounce back the electrons fired at them by the microscope while the lighter carbon atoms of the paper and ink do not.

The officer in question thought he had spotted the offending lorry while out on his beat, wrote the registration number down on his hand and ran to the nearest telephone box to call it in to check with the station. It was the wrong number and the marks on his hand were erased later that night in the officer's bathtub. The next day a telex came into the station where he was based from police in the north of England seeking a hijacked vehicle.

Feeling that the number of the lorry he had written down might be that of the hijacked truck he tried to recall the digits, without luck. Then he was sent to the

Dr. Williams cites the case of the assasi-nation attempt upon the Israeli ambassador to Britain in 1982 as one of those which would never have led to a conviction if it had not been for the great strides forward in forensic technology. When the accused, Hussein Said, stood in the witness box in February 1983 he was confident of an acquittal. The man he had shot, Shlomo Argov, was too ill from his wounds to give evidence, the police had discharged their own firearms at the scene and Said had said nothing under interrogation to incriminate himself. Traces of gunpowder and gun oil found on Said after the attempt could, said his lawyers, just as easily have come from the police weapons.

A TRICKY SITUATION

Dr. Williams called it a "classic forensic conundrum. We had the problem of associ-ating this arrested man first of all with the discarded weapon used to shoot the ambas-sador and with the ambassador himself. And we had to somehow discard all possi-bility that the evidence found on the accused had come from the police guns."

When a gun is fired what happens is that the firing pin strikes the primer at the base of the cartridge, detonating it by percussion and setting off the main propellant. The gases given off condense and particles of solid material settle on the person firing the gun. They are of a very particular type, containing a combination of three elements – lead, barium and antimony. This combi-nation is found, and found only, in particles left behind from gunfire. Dr. Williams set the Met's scanning electron microscope to work to solve the puzzle.

"Analysis of the guns, ammunition and residue samples taken from the suspect, the police and the victim told a remarkable story," said Dr. Williams, who described the whole sleuthing process for this puzzle as "elegant". The particle analysis showed traces of mercury on the discarded weapon, the one the prosecution said had been used to shoot the ambassador. Mercury also showed up on the suspect and on the flesh and clothing of the ambassador. The com-bination of residue particles, it turned out, was characteristic of ammunition from Iron Curtain countries, China and the Middle East. Europe and America hadn't used mer-cury in ordnance for 30 years. Analysis of police weapons and clothing showed only the trinity of barium, antimony and lead.

"None of these were found on the assailant or on the gun that had been fired," said Dr. Williams. "So we eliminated the possibility that the police, in their arresting of the man, had passed on firearms residue from their own weapons. So there was a clear-cut link, and a very elegant link, between assailant, victim and weapon." The jury returned a verdict of guilty on Said – another victory that was due to the leaps and bounds made by forensic boffins.

MERCURY SHOWED UP ON THE DISCARDED WEAPON, THE SUSPECT AND ON THE FLESH AND CLOTHING OF THE AMBASSADOR

"THERE WAS A CLEAR-CUT LINK, AND A VERY ELEGANT LINK, BETWEEN ASSAILANT, VICTIM AND WEAPON," SAID DR WILLIAMS

Below: *A slow-motion picture of a shotgun cartridge spewing out its lethal contents. Such minute details aid police in determining from what distance victims were shot.*

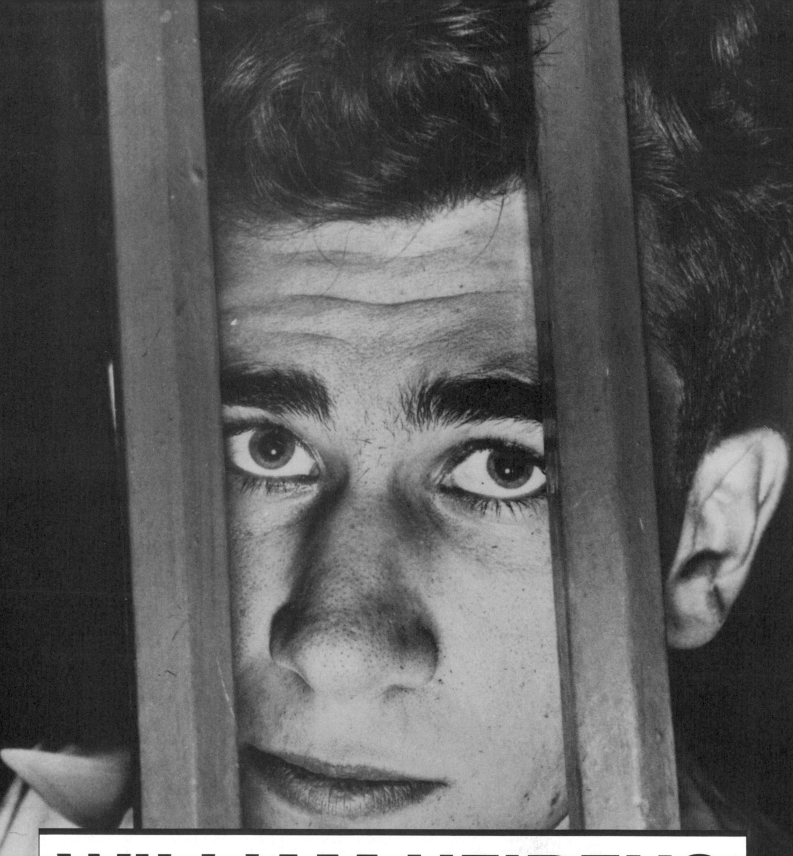

WILLIAM HEIRENS
The Mama's Boy

William Heirens pitted his evil wits against the best that law enforcement could throw at him after committing crimes against defenceless victims. He lost his perverse battle with the law, thanks to the advancements in forensic science that pinned him to his crimes like a butterfly to a board.

I t was a balmy day in Chicago on June 3 1945, the breeze coming from Lake Michigan affording little relief to the residents of the huge metropolis. Many sought shelter on that afternoon in movie theatres – one of the few places, aside from the huge slaughterhouses which gave the city its nickname "Hog Town" – that had air conditioning. Attractive widow Josephine Alice Ross was thinking of going to the cinema that day too, but instead stayed at home... a decision that was to cost her her life. The nude body of the 43-year-old woman was found later on her bed, her skirt and a nylon stocking tied around her throat. But she hadn't died from strangulation – huge knife wounds covered her face and neck and it was later determined that she bled to death. The most peculiar aspect of the crime scene to detectives was the blood-soaked towels and her own pyjamas lying in a tub of water in the bathroom. Captain Frank Reynolds of the Chicago police department glanced at his men and said: "The killer washed the blood from the body. This is a new one on me."

The body of the dead woman was found at lunchtime that day by her 17-year-old daughter who had left the apartment shortly before 9.00am, so she had been murdered in a four-hour time period. There was no sexual assault on the body, no money was missing, no valuables taken. It all pointed to a frenzied, motiveless murder. The killer, police learned, would have had no trouble entering the apartment as she never kept

THE NUDE BODY OF THE WOMAN WAS FOUND LATER ON HER BED, HER SKIRT AND A NYLON STOCKING TIED AROUND HER THROAT

Opposite: *The face of pure evil stares through the bars of a cell. There was to be no escape for William Heirens.*

Below: *Josephine Ross (left) and Frances Brown (right), two of Heirens' victims.*

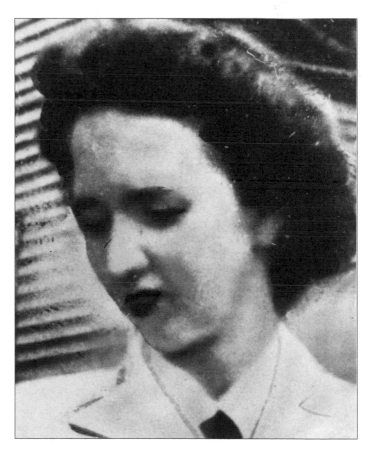

Above: *A monster's victim, six-year-old Suzanne Degnan (left), seen here with her sister Elizabeth.*

SCRAWLED ON A WALL WAS A MESSAGE: "FOR HEAVEN'S SAKE CATCH ME BEFORE I KILL MORE. I CANNOT CONTROL MYSELF"

the door locked. And he was a methodical man – he had wiped the place clean of all fingerprints. He was so thorough the forensic experts didn't even find a print of her daughter or her sister who also lived there.

Yet on that first day they questioned two eyewitnesses, a janitor and a neighbour, who swore that they had seen a hatless young man walking into the building wearing a white sweater and dark trousers with his hair brushed back in a pompadour. One saw him enter, the other saw him leaving around two hours later – the delay was probably the result of his obsessive cleaning of the apartment.

Months went by and no suspect was turned up. The initial police theory that the man was a lover of Mrs. Ross who had lost his head in an argument could not be substantiated. Every man who knew the widow was questioned and eliminated from the investigation. But as time went on several more apparently meaningless, equally brutal attacks were made on women in the city.

On October 1 Veronica Hudzinski, 19, was shot with a revolver and barely lived.

Four days later Army nurse Evelyn Peterson was beaten unconscious in her home and was in the process of being strangled with electrical flex when the man suddenly stopped and asked if he could get her a doctor. He walked calmly from the apartment as she clung to life… but not before he wiped the place clean of dabs. A second unexplained shooting happened on December 5, and again the victim managed to escape with just minor injuries.

But five days later the body of 30-year-old Frances Brown was found draped over a washtub at the residential Pine Crest Hotel. Near the body, scrawled on a wall in her bright red lipstick, was a message: "For Heaven's Sake Catch Me Before I Kill More. I Cannot Control Myself." The victim had been shot, strangled, and her face mutliated with deep knife wounds. And her body had been washed of blood and the room wiped down meticulously to remove all fingerprints. She too had not been sexually molested.

A VITAL MISTAKE

Yet this time the killer made one slight slip. He had indeed been methodical in removing the fingerprints, but not methodical enough. On the left jamb of the bathroom door was a print of one finger. It was a seemingly hopeless task matching this one print to an individual as the Chicago police department filed and classified fingerprints according to the dominant characteristics of all five fingers. Nevertheless a police sergeant named Thomas Laffey was assigned the mindbending task of sorting through 1,250,000 sets of prints. If nothing else, public opinion needed to be satisfied that everything was being done.

But four weeks later the horror of the murders and woundings receded in the public consciousness with the kidnapping of six-year-old Suzanne Degnan. Suzanne had gone to bed on the evening of January 7 1946 in her parents' home a mile from the Ross murder site – and the next morning her father James, going into her bedroom, found the window was open and the bed empty.

Two policemen cruising the area in a patrol car were there within a minute, one of them finding on the floor of her room a note that read: "Get $20,000 Ready & Wait For Word. Do Not Notify FBI or Police. Bills in 5's and 10's." On the reverse side of the note in capitals was the threat: "BURN THIS FOR HER SAFETY."

With police help, her father made a desperate and heart-rending appeal on the city radio station to return the little girl. The police didn't initially tell him, but the clues at the crime scene pointed to the fact that her abductor could be the same maniac responsible for the murders and woundings. There was a single print on the note that didn't correspond to the print found at the last murder… but did correspond with a fragment of fingerprint that a second search of the first murder scene had thrown up! Police were downcast and certain that a man of such a psychotic nature might already have murdered the little girl.

Later that night, as her father's wireless appeal was repeated over the city airwaves, two detectives lifted the lid of a storm drain. Floating in the sewer water beneath was the head of Suzanne. The rest of her body was missing.

During the next four hours Mayor Kelly had to repeatedly go on the air to assure Chicagoans of their safety. In the same period the other parts of little Suzanne's body were found in various sewers across the city. Something approaching panic gripped the usually stoical citizens of Chicago, many of whom protested outside the police department headquarters. Yet some progress was already being made in the hunt for the killer even as they shouted threats of violence.

EYES OF TRUTH

A witness was found who could have seen the murderer; a former Marine had been parked in his car near the Degnan home talking to his girlfriend when he saw a young man walk by with a shopping bag. The shopping bag was later found containing parts of the little girl's dismembered body. An intensive search of the region

> FLOATING IN THE SEWER BENEATH WAS THE HEAD OF SUZANNE. THE REST OF HER BODY WAS MISSING

Below: *Mr and Mrs James Degnan, the strain showing in their tired eyes, wait for news of their little girl.*

Above: *Bones sifted from the ashes of an incinerator in Chicago – the incinerator that Heirens used as his DIY crematorium for his victims.*

turned up a small piece of twisted wire on which were found three head hairs that matched Suzanne's. A handkerchief was wrapped round one end of the wire – a hanky bearing the initials 3168-S. Sherman. It was customary for soldiers at the time to mark their possessions with the last four digits of their serial numbers. A search was launched to find the owner.

THE EXPERTS' ESTIMATE

As the hunt was on, forensic experts determined that Suzanne had died between 12.30 and 1.00am, strangled with the piece of wire that was found with the handkerchief. There were traces of coal dust on her feet and in her hair roots. Other than that, various parts of the body appeared to have been washed after they had been cut away. But the clue of the coal was later to prove significant in catching the killer.

Detectives believed that the coal dust indicated the girl had been dissected in a

---

DETECTIVES BELIEVED THAT THE COAL DUST INDICATED THE GIRL HAD BEEN DISSECTED IN A CELLAR

---

cellar. The next morning police began house-to-house searches of all cellars in the neighbourhood of Suzanne's home. In the afternoon they appeared to strike gold. In the basement of a four-storey house on Winthrop Avenue, just a block from her home, detectives found faint smears of blood in the basement and in a drain trap discovered bits of flesh and blonde hairs.

A woman tenant in the apartment directly above said she had been disturbed at 2.30am by someone in the laundry room running water. A new shipment of coal had come that morning and when detectives moved it they discovered bloodstains from the bin on the floor.

A locker belonging to one of the tenants had been forced open. Inside it had been the shopping bag which was eventually found floating in the sewer with parts of Suzanne's body inside. The man didn't live in the building as a door was found forced. Later police would find out that the handkerchief belonged to an innocent sailor called Sherman whose home had been burgled. They now believed they were looking for a thief who had been transformed into an unstoppable, murderous beast.

Harry Gold, a man who had been on holiday in Florida when the Suzanne murder occurred, returned home to find his apartment – one that overlooked the dead girl's home – ransacked. They believed the culprit had gone to the apartment on a burglary and on an impulse had seen the little girl and decided to enter the apartment for another moneymaking scheme – except that his own berserk impulses were unable to stop him ultimately from killing her.

The guilty man's arrest, despite one of the largest police efforts in Chicago history, finally came through pure chance – even though it wasn't for some hours that they realised that the man they had could be the maniac they were seeking. A youthful burglar was caught after being chased by police. The sprightly thief was fleet-footed and gave a long chase, turning to fire on his pursuer. But an off duty police officer final-

> THEY WERE LOOKING FOR A THIEF WHO HAD BEEN TRANSFORMED INTO AN UNSTOPPABLE, MURDEROUS BEAST

Below: *A telegram from the FBI showing that Heirens' palm prints matched those on the ransom note in the Degnan child case.*

ly hurled three flowerpots on to his head and he offered no more resistance. Papers on the youth identified him as William Heirens, a 17-year-old student at the Chicago University.

PREVIOUS FORM

A check on police records showed that he had been arrested in 1942, when he was 13, for carrying a pistol. Other arrests were for a string of burglaries – six homes which he torched after looting. Heirens was taken to a prison hospital for wounds sustained during his arrest. While he recovered, police seized a large arsenal of weapons at the house where he lived with his parents in a city suburb. These included a rifle, a .25 calibre pistol, two .38 revolvers and four more pistols and a rifle hidden under tarpaulin on the roof.

This seemed encouraging enough, but Heirens lay in a coma in hospital. As he remained unconscious a search of his room on the university campus turned up stolen

Above: *Three detectives who did mankind a favour – the ones who caught Heirens. They are Detective Abner Cunningham (standing), Det. William Owens (left) and Det. Tiffen Constant.*

Right: *Heirens, flanked by his mother and father and surrounded by lawmen.*

MINUTE PARTICLES OF DUST ON HIS SHOES MATCHED THE DUST IN THE CELLAR WHERE THE LITTLE GIRL WAS CUT UP

property from dozens of burglaries – including items taken from the Gold home opposite the murdered girl's house. But it didn't link him directly with the murders – not until a dirty pair of shoes was handed to the forensic department that had collated scenes-of-crime clues. An examination of minute particles of dust on the soles of his shoes matched exactly the coal dust found in the cellar where the little girl was cut up.

A police department expert, Brian Connolly, said: "There are hundreds of grades of coal, thousands of sub-grades. But using a chemical solution and a machine which span the dust particles from the shoes and the cellar we were able to determine, without question, that they had come from the same source. Whatever else he did or didn't do, those shoes and the person in them had been in that cellar. And the samples were all taken while he was unaware. There was more. Underneath the killer's fingernails were minute quantities of soap. These were removed as he slept and placed through similar testing at a laboratory which determined that it was exact-

Above: *Carried from his hospital bed by detectives, Heirens is pictured en route to his appointment with a lie detector machine.*

ly the same kind of soap which he had used to wash the chopped-up corpse with."

For three days more, police kept this information from him, preferring a confession to relying solely on forensic evidence. Too often before it had been thrown out of court by laymen jurors who were medieval in their outlook when it came to "new fangled" devices such as acid tests, solutions and spectrographs.

When he finally came around from his "coma" – a feigned state which police think was a device to bide him some thinking time – he rambled on about another man called George Murman being responsible for the crimes. He agreed to go under sodium pentathol – truth serum – an experiment that backfired badly for the police.

AN INTERESTING DRUG

The injection of sodium pentathol induces the patient to a state of narcosynthesis, blotting out the active mind, freeing the subconscious state to answer questions. Most times the person who receives the drug cannot help himself in telling the truth. But Heirens spoke of the mystery man George with such clarity and conviction that the police and FBI thought they had blown it. The stenographic record of the polygraph machine linked up to him seemed to suggest that every answer he gave, however implausible, was the truth. Only the undisputed forensic evidence gave the police hope of proceeding with the prosecution. Detective Chief Storms said: "We could have nailed him on burglary charges no problem, but the truth test stymied us. We needed that forensic badly."

An extensive search across America, utilising police files, FBI data, servicemen's records, missing persons' records and social security numbers failed to find any record of a George Murman, the mystery man that Heirens said he befriended in a hotel in Chicago shortly before the little girl was murdered.

Police were willing to risk a prosecution on the strength of the forensic evidence alone when Heirens was forced to undergo a psychiatric examination. Mind doctors believed that Heirens had managed to sink into a deep psychotic state in which he possessed an alter ego – George – that had carried out the killings.

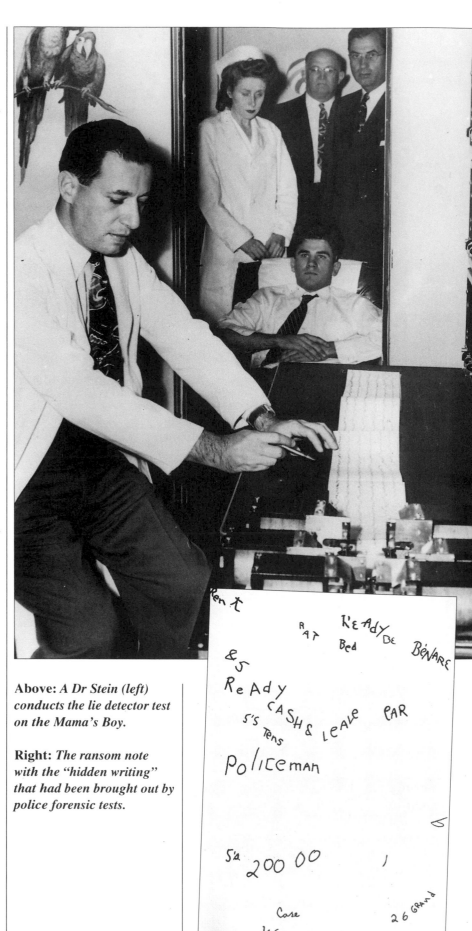

Above: *A Dr Stein (left) conducts the lie detector test on the Mama's Boy.*

Right: *The ransom note with the "hidden writing" that had been brought out by police forensic tests.*

He was indicted on a total of 27 burglaries and four woundings as a means of holding him in jail while enquiries continued. There was still no proof of linking him with the murders unless he confessed. There seemed little chance of a direct confession and so the case was to hinge on the soap and coal dust.

Yet on August 6 the same impulses that had snapped to change him from a burglar to murder, snapped to turn him from innocent to guilty. He admitted killing the two women and the child, saying he derived sexual satisfaction from the deaths even though he didn't rape them or otherwise sexually molest them. "I got a real thrill," he said. "It was more the breaking in than the murders. I just lost it. But I never touched them in that way." He could not say why he had lingered for two hours each time over the deaths of his victims, nor why he had washed them.

REAL FANTASY

And he finally admitted that George was a figment of his own imagination. "To me he's very real," said Heirens. "He exists. You can accept George as being me but, well, it's hard to explain. A couple of times I had talks with him. I suppose I was really talking to myself. I wrote lots of notes to him which I kept."

It was during his confession that psychiatrists noted continued references to his mother, about how he always wanted to please her throughout his life and how he always seemed to fail to do so. Hence the nickname "Mama's Boy" which stuck with him through the trial and the rest of his days behind bars.

On September 7 1946 he pleaded guilty to the murders and was ordered to be held for life without any possibility of parole. Shortly after entering the Illinois State Penitentiary he became an unruly, troublesome prisoner who was often in trouble for fighting and infracting other prison rules. He was again examined by psychiatrists who deemed him insane and he was transferred to a mental institution similar to Britain's Broadmoor.

William Heirens tore up the rule book for serial killers. Men who kill mature women don't go after children. Burglars don't become serial killers. Burglars don't

HE ADMITTED KILLING THE TWO WOMEN AND THE CHILD, SAYING HE DERIVED SEXUAL SATISFACTION FROM THE DEATHS

Below: *Smiling and casual, this portrait of Heirens was snapped just after his attempted suicide.*

become snipers who shoot women. The only thread running through his crimes was the strange washing-up afterwards of the bodies which brings the police to an ironic postscript to his evil reign. For forensic scientist David Steinman said: "Had he washed the bodies in warm water instead of cold – and wiped his shoes with warm water instead of cold – he would have removed the forensic evidence. That in turn would have made police loathe to charge him and in turn he would have served some time for burglary and been on the streets of Chicago within a decade. We are lucky he didn't have warm water."

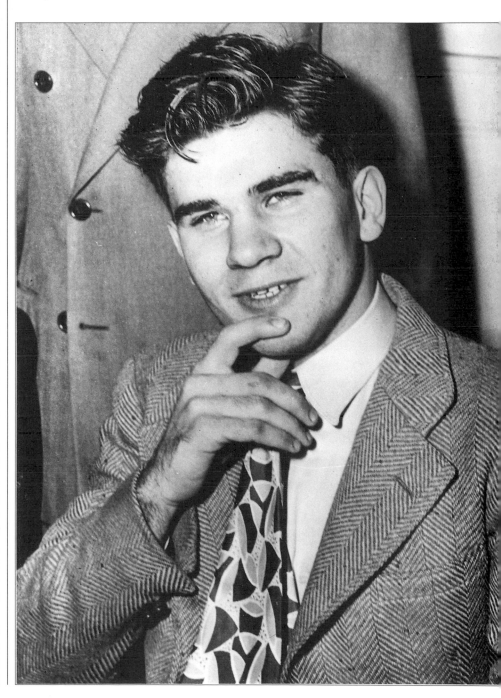

KAREN PRICE
Face Value

The case of Karen Price stands unmatched in British criminal history. It was a work of such intensive labour, painstaking forensic investigation, brilliant deduction and awesome teamwork that it deserves to stand apart from all other cases in this or any other century.

Thanks to the brilliance shown by the team in identifying murder victim Karen Price from nothing more than her fleshless skull her killers were caught and imprisoned. One prominent academic said that the case "significantly advanced forensic science in this country by 20 years". More than that, it enabled justice to be done and for the family of the missing girl to finally – more than ten years after she disappeared – place her remains in a grave where she could rest in peace and they could mourn her with respect.

Karen Price was murdered a decade earlier but the corpse of the woman who was to become so valuable in the forensic fight against crime was actually discovered on the afternoon of December 7 1989. Workmen Keith Lloyd, Syd Williams, Billy David and Paul Bodenham had been gutting a house in Fitzhamon Embankment, Cardiff, an address bordering a seedy red light area of the city. Number 29, a gothic three-storey building, was being converted into flats as was the custom with many turn-of-the-century homes in this bedsit area of the Welsh capital. On this afternoon, as dusk was falling, it became apparent to the men that the trench they had been digging in the garden for a new wastepipe was not going to be deep enough. Lloyd jumped into the excavation to dig another

six inches down – but his pickaxe head hit a soft object. Closer inspection revealed it to be a carpet tied with electrical flex. When the cigar-shaped object was removed and the flex untied a human skeleton was revealed as the contents.

Within an hour the area had been sealed off as a murder site. Forensic experts collected soil samples while a police pathologist examined the remains. Most of the flesh had gone but rotting particles of clothing still draped off some of the bones. Blonde curls were visible around the skull and a pair of gilt earrings were found nearby. It became clear from the most senior officer present to the most junior rookie that identifying such a body would be a mammoth task. Detective Chief Superintendent John Williams, head of South Wales CID, viewed the body the day

Opposite: *Karen Price's body was found a decade after she went missing.*

Below: *It was when renovations were being carried out at this house that the Woman Without a Face was discovered.*

*Above: **Richard Neave, a man who has built reconstructions of numerous historical figures.***

DET. CHF. SUPT. WILLIAMS
PLEDGED "TO CALL IN
EVERY 'OLOGIST IN THE
BOOK TO SOLVE
THE CRIME"

it was found and said: "I didn't think it was possible to reconstruct a face from what I saw." In fact the medical and forensic experts set out to accomplish nothing less than the total reconstruction of a long-dead body. It was to be an extraordinary alliance of pathology, odontology – the study of teeth – forensic tests on the clothing, anthropology, entomology – the study of insects – a brilliant medical illustrator and geneticists. Each of them deserves a slice of the credit in bringing the murderers of this young girl to book.

The first stage in the investigation was the police decision to treat her death as murder. Det. Chf. Supt. Williams said he was satisfied, even before hearing from the pathologist, that a body being buried in a garden was clearly due to foul play and pledged to "call in every 'ologist in the book the solve the crime". On the evening of the day that the corpse was discovered it was laid out in the morgue at the Cardiff Royal Infirmary for inspection by Dr. Bernard Knight, professor of pathology at the Welsh Institute of Forensic Medicine. He determined that the skeleton was of a young white woman, about 5ft. 4ins. tall. The doctor said analysis of the bones suggested a girl in her mid-teens but he had not determined the cause of death.

While the pathological team examined the corpse the soil that it had lain in was coming under the intense scrutiny of Nicholas Coles, a Welsh archaeological expert. Unfortunately, his examination of the grave site was fruitless because much of the soil had already been removed by workmen before they had jumped into the ditch to deepen it.

A MACABRE INVESTIGATION

The next cog in the machinery of identification was the Home Office forensic laboratory at Chepstow, Gwent. Most of the material had rotted, but the clay in which she had lain had preserved some remnants. Working from the material which survived the scientists were able to determine that her bra was a size 36B and had been manufactured by the Shadowline company in Liverpool and sold in Cardiff through a company called Mrs. Knickers. This was an important piece of the puzzle – as police liaised with missing persons' bureaux over the number of missing teenaged girls in Britain it seemed likely that she was local and had purchased the items there. Her sweatshirt was size 18, manufactured by the American firm Levi for the British market and sold around 1980 – placing her death at some time in the last decade.

The skull was delivered to the Natural History Museum in London where anthropologists Dr. Christopher Stringer and Theya Molleson examined it from every angle, measured it and fed the data into a computer programme used to identify 2,500 different skull types from around the world. They determined the girl's skull was from a caucasian female.

Further examination of the teeth and jaw made them speculate that she was probably not an indigenous Briton – widening the net to immigrants and visitors to the

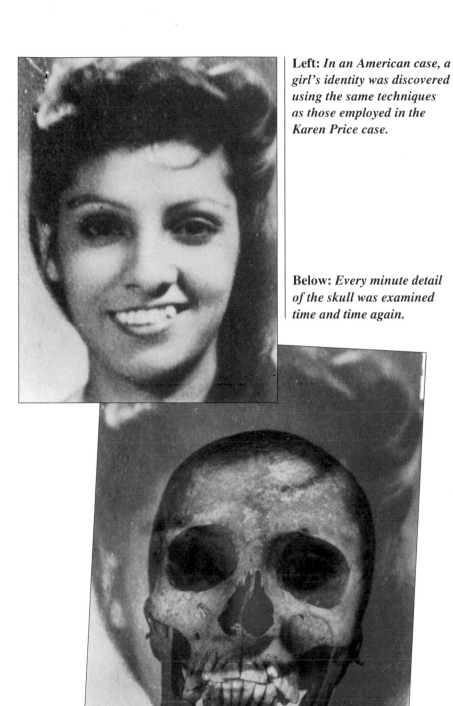

Left: *In an American case, a girl's identity was discovered using the same techniques as those employed in the Karen Price case.*

Below: *Every minute detail of the skull was examined time and time again.*

country. The skull became the focus of the inquiry – it was undamaged and from it much more could be gleaned than from any other part of the skeleton.

Dr. David Whittaker, the forensic dental adviser to the Home Office, used a tried and trusted method to try to gauge her age from the teeth. He took a cross section of one tooth and, rather like determining the age of a tree by counting the rings of a sawed trunk, speculated "80 per-cent" certain that she was 15-and-a-half when she

---

HE MEASURED HOW LONG THE CADAVER HAD LAIN IN THE GROUND BY EXAMINING DEAD INSECT TISSUE FOUND WITH HER

---

died. He also found traces of blood in capillaries in the skull. These tiny veins are usually empty at death, except in cases of violent death; he speculated that she had met her end at the hands of a strangler. He also remarked that the poor quality of the dental work indicated that she had spent time under the care of a foreign dentist, but he couldn't pin down a country.

HUMAN COMPLICATIONS

A 70-strong police team meanwhile embarked on all the routine, necessary enquiries related to such a murder. It was estimated by Williams that some 700 people had lived in the house and the adjoining one during the decade, many of them drifters who stayed for only a short while. But no-one quizzed seemed to remember a fair-haired teenager. Williams began to sense that as the case progressed he was going to have to rely more and more on the "boffins" who were methodically trying to find out who Miss X was.

The next person to be called in provided some of the most fascinating clues. In December 1989 and January the following year the skull, soil samples, skeletal remains and clothing particles were examined by Dr. Zakeria Erzincliogu, a brilliant Cambridge University professor specialising in entomology – the lives of insects.

He was able to measure how long the cadaver had lain in the ground by examining the dead insect tissue found with her. Woodlice, phorid flies – tissue-eating insects – and bluebottle larvae, the eggs of flies. The first two indicated that the girl had been buried in the ground for five years at least, placing her death before 1984, which corresponded with the clothing found on her.

More importantly, the bluebottle eggs could only have been laid on the corpse when it was exposed to air and in this he estimated that her body had been unburied for two days after her murder.

It was all leading somewhere but no-one knew quite where. That is when one of the police officers recalled reading about a renowned artist who had been helping to build a plaster-cast of a victim of the 1987 Kings Cross Underground fire who had remained unidentified since then. Williams thought it was worth contacting Richard

Neave, a 54-year-old medical illustrator who was based at Manchester University. Neave's skill came in re-constructing human faces based just on the shape, size and contours of their skulls. He started on the face of Miss X by making a plastercast of the skull and gradually built up features using modelling clay.

He was the first to admit that putting the features on a skull is the part "where art and science meet" and that mistakes can occur. But probably there is no-one in the world with his skill or attention to detail. During a lengthy career he has put the faces on long-dead Egyptian mummies, a murder victim whose killers were caught thanks to his efforts and the ancient ruler Phillip of Macedon.

He gained his expertise in human anatomy by watching surgical procedures and dissections at medical universities across Britain and has honed his skills to a finer-than-fine art. He saw the task of re-creating Miss X as a great forensic challenge and the skull was placed in a cardboard box and driven to him by police.

Below: *All the efforts of the investigators were to prove worthwhile for the comfort they brought to Karen's family. They also made British crime history.*

PAINSTAKING CONSTRUCTION

Neave received the skull on December 18 and set to work. He used anatomical sketchbooks while he started to "build" the face, muscle by muscle, feeling with his fingers where the flesh, bone, muscle and sinew would have been on every square centimetre of her face. He uses exact measurements on muscle depth and skin type based on figures of real people and applies them to whatever age he is working to.

It is very methodical work that has to be done carefully piece by piece because, he says, "I am not a sculptor making a piece of art-work – it is a scientific construction." In the case of Miss X he said: "I used all the information that was gathered from experts. You have to remember that she was only 15-and-a-half, healthy, lots of elasticity in her face. Life won't have driven a truck over her face."

Nose and lips could be done first because the skull doesn't dictate their size or thickness. Then he continued his moulding of the eyebrows, forehead, cheeks, chin and ears until, in two days, he was satisfied with what he had in front of him.

On January 8 1990 Det. Chf. Supt. Williams called a press conference in Cardiff during which photographs of the reconstruction were handed out to representatives of TV and newspapers. The photograph was also made into a "have you seen this girl?" poster which was issued to police stations all over Britain for distribution at social halls, railway and bus stations and other places where crowds congregate.

The face was of a young girl with slightly flared nose and straggly hair. But it was a complete face, a complete human being, not a shadowy artist's impression which have often proved worse than useless in tracking down criminals and missing persons.

The speed with which the girl's identity came after that press conference was truly astonishing. Forty eight hours after the nationwide appeals went out two social workers in Cardiff contacted police to say they believed the girl looked like a young runaway called Karen Price, aged 15.

She had been in care when she went missing in 1981, said the informants, and were emphatic it was her. Other names of missing girls were offered up too, but they were all traced.

FINAL CONFIRMATION

It then fell on police to find Karen Price's dental records, which turned up in a Cardiff dentist's storeroom in late January 1990 and were sent to the expert Whittaker for analysis. He said there was no doubt that the dead girl was Karen Price. Further confirmation came when Dr. Peter Vanezis, a senior lecturer in forensic medicine at the London Hospital, was sent a photo of Karen. Using the latest video-computer technology he electronically superimposed the photograph of Karen on to her skull and got an almost perfect match.

The corpse had a name and she had a family who would now be able to mourn for her properly.

Between January and July 1990, as police efforts concentrated on finding her killers, further forensic work was carried out. Police were determined to get a DNA match through genetic fingerprinting – which would prove scientifically it was her. This was obtaned by sending a bone sample from Karen's femur to Dr. Erik Hagelberg of the Institute of Molecular Medicine at Oxford University.

Her test involved chilling the bone with liquid nitrogen, then crushing it to extract the DNA. Professor Alec Jeffreys, of the department of genetics at Leicester University – the man who invented DNA fingerprinting – compared the DNA with blood samples taken from Karen's parents, who had been traced in the intervening time. Despite being used on bones of such an age and subject to decay, he was able to say better than "99.9 per-cent that these are the remains of Karen Price".

The life of Karen Price was, police discovered, an unhappy one. Her father Michael and her mother Anita Nicholaidis were divorced when she was a child and she went into the care of the Glamorgan social services when she was 10. Her mother's Greek-Cypriot roots accounted for Karen's teeth appearing "foreign". Not long before her 16th birthday she was moved to an assessment centre for troublesome children where decisions were to be made about her future. But she absconded on July 8 1981, joining the legions of missing children who make up a lost army in Britain.

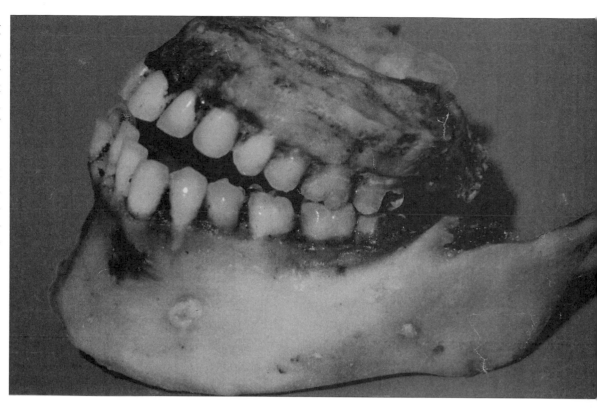

Above: *The teeth of Karen Price – although it would take far more than her dentures to identify her.*

THE CORPSE HAD A NAME AND SHE HAD A FAMILY WHO WOULD NOW BE ABLE TO MOURN FOR HER PROPERLY

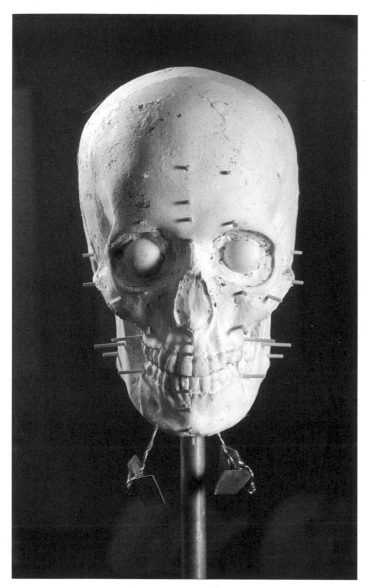

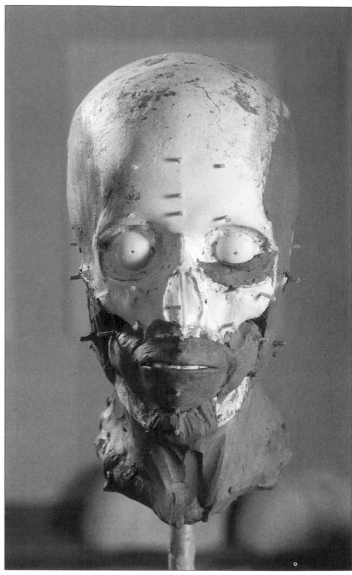

There was no police hunt for her and, apparently, no-one to weep for her. She simply became just another statistic in an ever-lengthening book.

The police issued further appeals, concentrating once more on people who had one time been resident of the house where the body was buried. Sifting through records they found that an Alan Charlton had once been resident in the bottom flat – the flat from which the off-cut of carpet came that was used to wrap Karen's body. Charlton lived in Bridgewater, Somerset, and had recently been released from a jail sentence for attempting to rape a 55-year-old woman. It was interesting to the police, but inconclusive.

But soon after he was interviewed a TV appeal went out for more information and a young girl who had been at school with Karen came forward. She said a a man

Above: *The model of the skull begins to take shape with wooden skewers inserted to determine the correct depth of flesh and skin. It was a laborious process but one that was to pay enormous dividends.*

caled Idris Ali had boasted that he knew Karen. He was eventually interviewed and, unexpectedly during what the police considered a routine suspect-elimination session, he broke down and confessed: "I killed her. I am sorry."

Ali fingered an accomplice – the attempted rapist Charlton who had been seen by lawmen previously. He also implicated another girl, whose identity was witheld at their subsequent trial, who knew about the killing but escaped prosecution because of what she knew. She was to prove a star witness at the trial of the two men. It turned out that Ali had persuaded Karen to become a prostitute while the two were together at a school for disadvantaged children. Ali became her pimp and pimp to the other girl, simply known as Miss X at the trial. Charlton came into the scene when he said he could organise porno

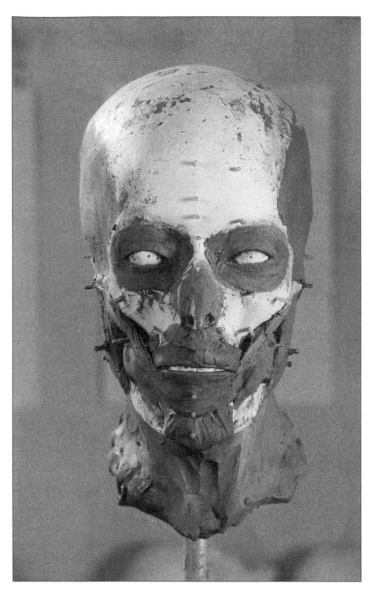 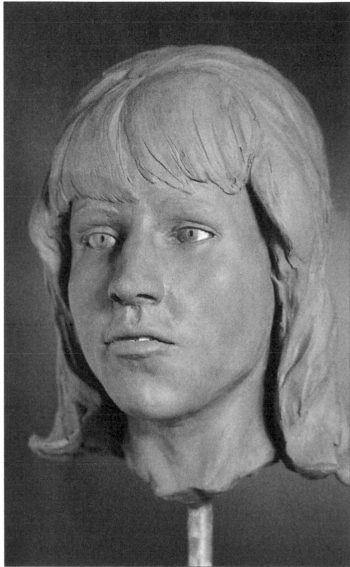

movies and drugs in his basement flat at… Fitzhamon Embankment. The girls would procure the clients and they would all share in the profits.

But something went wrong. Miss X testified that Karen refused to be photographed naked. She quarrelled with the men and Charlton exploded, beating her to death in the basement. Her body was left exposed for four days – hence the bluebottle larvae found on the skeleton – and she was later interred by Ali and Charlton in the back garden. After so many years they figured their secret was safe.

But in a five week trial which ended at Cardiff Crown Court on February 26 1991 justice finally caught up with them when they were jailed for life. After Mr. Justice Hose had sentenced the prisoners he paid special compliments to the unique alliance of law enforcement, forensic and scientific

Above: *Slowly but surely the model began to resemble less a Hallowe'en caricature and more the face of a beautiful girl whose life was brutally and cruelly snuffed out. Finally, this sculpture was unveiled to the world, and the girl who had no dignity in death was finally accorded the full rights of a Christian burial.*

people who had collaborated so unselfishly in the process of finding out the identity of the corpse. Det. Chf. Supt. Williams, who has since left the force, paid particular tribute to Neave, whose masterful reconstruction of Karen's face was, in his opinion, integral in finding out who she was. He said: "I don't know whether we would have done it without him.

"It was of the utmost importance that the identity of the girl was corroborated beyond doubt. That was the first objective. It was a bonus that we were able to charge two people with murder. Co-operation between the police and the forensic experts reached new heights and in my 33 years as a police officer this case was unique."

Karen Price was given a decent, Christian burial. It was, perhaps, one of the few times in her short, sad life that she was truly recognised by society.

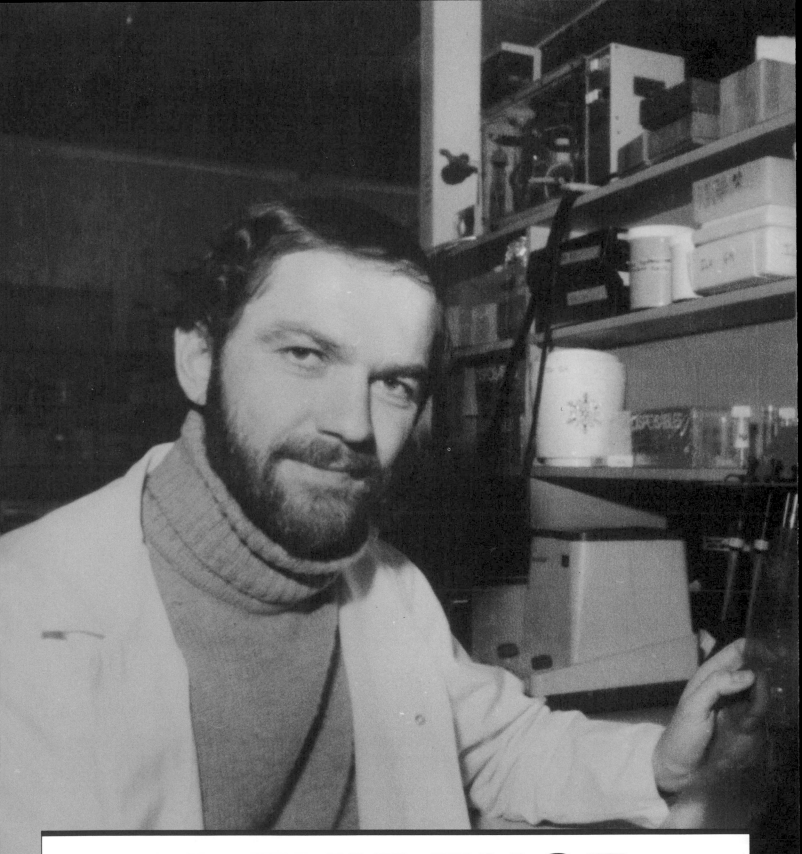

DNA EVIDENCE
Fingering Criminals

Professor Sir Alec Jeffreys of the University of Leicester stumbled upon the miracle of DNA fingerprinting while he was researching another subject. His brilliance has taken away all hiding places for criminals and advanced the detection of crime more than any other single discovery.

It was a revolutionary request that sparked an enormous amount of controversy. It came when police hunting the maniacal killer of two young girls stepped forward to say they would be "fingerprinting" 2,000 men of a single village in a bid to trap their man. But it wasn't fingerprinting in the normal sense, an ink pad and roller to take the dabs of every male over a certain age in the community. This was "genetic fingerprinting", the technique devised by a brilliant university professor that would compare the living tissue of a person with tissue samples found on the two dead schoolgirls.

The human DNA cannot lie and if the police had a match they also had their killer. There were complaints about civil liberty violations, wrangling from a major chemical company which laid claim to the licensing rights on the process and scepticism from certain old-fashioned lawmen who doubted whether such a new-fangled system could ever replace the old tried and

THE HUMAN DNA CANNOT LIE AND IF THE POLICE HAD A MATCH THEY ALSO HAD THEIR KILLER

Opposite: *Professor Sir Alec Jeffreys, discoverer of DNA.*

Below: *Taking a blood sample is all that is needed to begin DNA analysis.*

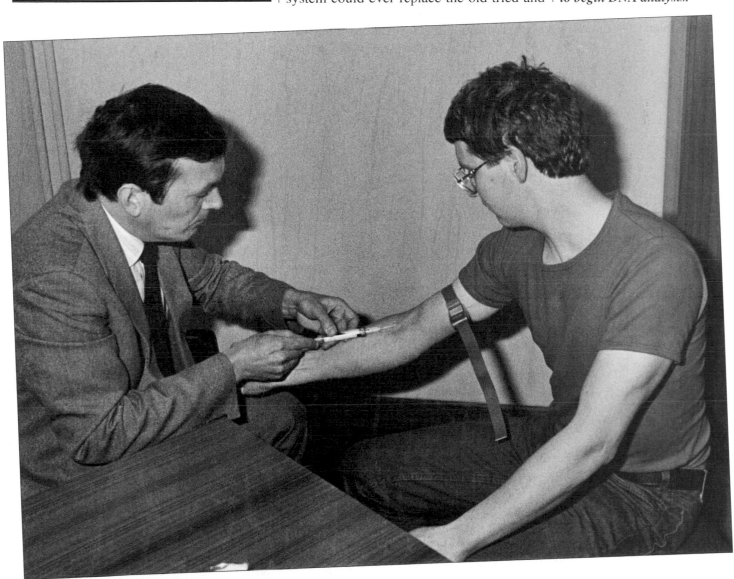

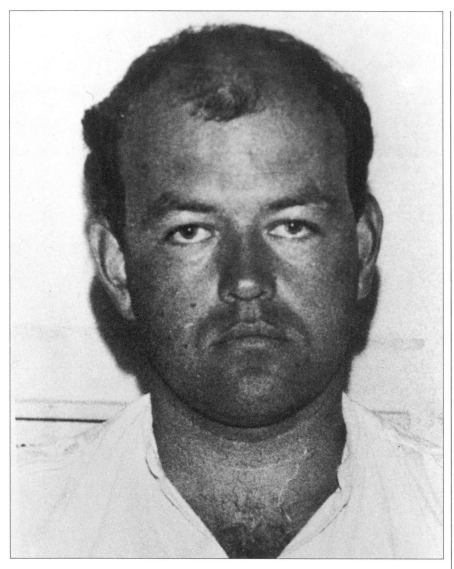

Above: *Colin Pitchfork, the brutal sex killer who sent a man in his place to give blood when he feared that the DNA test would find him out.*

Right: *Dawn Ashworth, one of Pitchfork's victims.*

THE MURDERS WERE OF SUCH DEPRAVITY THAT THEY MENTALLY SCARRED THE INHABITANTS OF THE REGION FOR YEARS

checks through the nationwide police computer to locate sex offenders and child murderers who had been released from jail near to the time of the killing. The enquiry dragged on for months with numerous CID officers manning an emergency incident room, desperately waiting for the one phone call or lead that would set them on the killer's trail. Eventually the investigation, although never closed, was forced to wind down as police manpower was needed for everyday crimefighting.

Three years later came the second brutal killing that bore many of the hallmarks of the first. Dawn Ashworth, also 15, was walking from a friend's home in Enderby to her own on July 31 1986 when she too failed to show up. Her body was found partially covered by hay three days later, near a footpath linking Enderby and Narborough. She too had been raped, but her physical injuries were worse than Lynda's; this time the killer had inflicted much more suffering in his attack.

A post-mortem examination disclosed horrifying injuries to her face, head and private parts. Senior officers at the scene of the crime were certain that the two attacks were linked – that somewhere in their quiet community was dwelling a monster who had urges that could not be controlled.

trusted policing methods. But the test worked 100 per-cent – sending the guilty man to prison for life and ensuring a place for DNA fingerprinting in criminal detection for decades to come.

The murders of the two girls came three years apart in Leicestershire, murders of such brutality and depravity that they mentally scarred the inhabitants of the region for years. Lynda Mann, 15, was the first to die. She set off from her home in Narborough, Leics., to see a friend in the nearby village of Enderby. It was the evening of November 21 1983 and the girls were going to spend an evening playing records and going over their schoolwork. But Lynda never arrived – her body was found the next morning near a footpath, raped and strangled with her own scarf, tied, police said, with "maniacal ferocity". There was a massive police hunt, nationwide appeals for help and the usual cross-

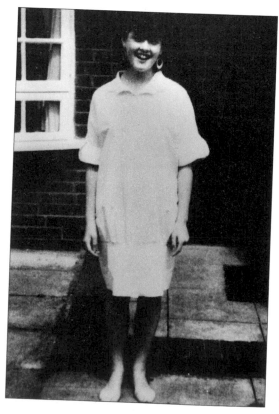

There was another huge manhunt, another mass appeal, anything that could home in on the killer who, the police were certain, was local. His knowledge of the footpaths around the village, near the M1 motorway and just five miles south-west of Leicester, led them to believe he could not be a stranger. Yet he had left no discernible clues at the crime scene... or had he? For in the years that spanned the murders a professor called Alec Jeffreys – later Sir Alec – had literally stumbled upon an astonishing new technique that would have profound consequences for crime and its detection all over the world.

AN ACCIDENTAL MIRACLE

Professor Jeffreys of the University of Leicester stumbled upon DNA fingerprinting while he was researching something else. DNA stands for deoxyribonucleic acid, found in the nuclei of all human body cells. Later Professor Jeffreys would say with characteristic understatement: "Like all good scientific breakthroughs, it was made while searching for something else and shows how important good basic university science is for Britain."

He was working on haemoglobin genes when he discovered that human DNA – the gossamer chemical strands of genetic material that determine individual body characteristics – are unique from person to person. Just as there are no two fingerprints alike, so there are no two specimens of human DNA alike. The possibilities for his discovery became limitless – in learning about the very building blocks of life, in the study of pregnancies and in the application of forensic science. By analysing these sections of DNA, called mini-satellites, a clear genetic fingerprint of a human being can be built up. "From a single drop of blood," said Dr. Jeffreys, "a bar code, unique to an individual, can be made.

"The test is highly accurate and is generally much better than present blood and other tests which often produce inconclusive results." The chiefs of police throughout Britain were not slow in recognising the fantastic potential of his discovery.

Detective Inspector Derek Pearse, leading the investigation into the two murders, first made use of Dr. Jeffrey's remarkable

technique to clear a suspect. Richard Buckland, a 17-year-old youth, was wrongly accused and charged with murdering Dawn. He had been seen hanging around the murder scene and was unable to explain his wherabouts on the night to the satisfaction of police officers. He was dramatically freed when DNA tests failed to link him to the murder because the DNA found on both bodies was the same – and he didn't possess it. It led the police toput into effect plans for the biggest DNA testing ever – across three villages in the area involving 2,000 men. So convinced were they that the killer was local they believed he was bound to be flushed out. Police emphasised that the tests were "purely voluntary" – but it was clear that the finger of suspicion would hover unerringly over those individuals who did not step forward.

Thousands of letters were sent out and testing sites arranged for this unique exper-

Above: *Police at the scene of the Lynda Mann murder. It would take an operation unprecedented in the history of crime detection to finally nail her killer.*

HE HAD STUMBLED UPON A TECHNIQUE THAT WOULD HAVE PROFOUND CONSEQUENCES FOR CRIME

iment in the science of crime fighting. But before it got off the ground there were problems. The chemical giant ICI claimed it owned the exclusive rights to the test and clearly felt it had expertise to offer.

In a statement in January 1987 the company said: "We know nothing about police plans to use our test. We are very concerned about this. We are the only people who have the right and capacity to carry out wide-scale testing using genetic fingerprinting but Leicester police haven't approached us at all."

ICI had indeed bought the copyright from Professor Jeffreys. There were also disquieting rumbles from some civil liberties quarters who felt personal rights could be trampled on in the mass test. But in time the problems were smoothed over and the government labs at Aldermaston were made ready to receive the tests.

Police wrote to men in the three villages between the ages of 17 and 33. Det. Insp. Pearse said: "The public response has so

Above: *The grieving parents of Dawn Ashworth, with Det. Chf. Supt. David Baker at their side, made a plea for the killer to give himself up.*

Right: *A policewoman dressed in clothes similar to Dawn's strolls near to where her body was found in a bid to jog the memories of potential witnesses.*

THOUSANDS OF LETTERS WERE SENT OUT AND TESTING SITES ARRANGED FOR A UNIQUE EXPERIMENT IN CRIME FIGHTING

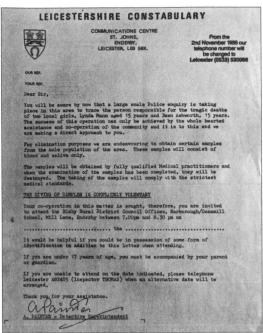

LEICESTERSHIRE CONSTABULARY

Left: *The letter sent to the male population in the area around the murder site.*

Below: *Ian Kelly, who had his blood tested in Colin Pitchfork's place.*

far been overwhelming. Hundreds of people have phoned the murder incident room to book a test, including students and servicemen. We haven't had one refusal so far." For some men, the tests were a great weight off their minds – they had become the target of suspicion and innuendo in a small community where neighbour was being turned against neighbour in the witch-hunt hysteria that surrounded the search for the killer. Groups of youths were among those volunteering together, so it could be seen that they were volunteering.

LIVING IN FEAR

But one man who had no intention of volunteering for anything was Colin Pitchfork. Pitchfork, of Littlethorpe – one of the villages earmarked for the test – had much to be afraid of, for it was he who had murdered the innocent schoolgirls to satisfy his perverted lust. A 27-year-old misfit with a history of exposing himself to women, he had been careful at the crimesites not to leave behind any items of clothing or other clues which might possibly lead detectives to his door. Yet he had read the newspapers; he knew that he could not possibly hope to beat the DNA test.

At the bakery where he worked Pitchfork told workmates he had previous convictions for indecent exposure before he married in 1981. He laughed them off, attributing them to high-spiritedness after

drinking, saying he wasn't "a pervert" but merely someone the police were out to get for what he considered a minor crime.

Using that as his theme he began to pester his workmates to step forward in his place. He tried to persuade them that the police would never know that he was at home if they went and gave their sample. "They want to fit me up for what happened before," he told them. "I would be a prime target for the police hoping to pin this on someone." The power of the DNA test was clearly great, even though it had not been performed on him. He offered one young man £50 to go in his place, then another £200. Finally, he persuaded a workmate named Ian Kelly, 23, to go instead and even coached him after hours at the bakery in how to forge his signature and memorise

"extraordinary lengths" to evade justice, but that in the end his partner in the deception had had second thoughts about it.

Judge Mr. Justice Otton had special praise for Dr. Jeffreys' breakthrough, saying: "In this case it not only led to the apprehension of the correct murderer, but also ensured that suspicion was removed from an innocent man.

"Had it not been for genetic fingerprinting, Colin Pitchfork might still be at liberty and that is too terrible a thing to contemplate." Kelly, of Leicester, admitting providing blood and saliva samples to police while pretending to be Pitchfork. He admitted conspiracy and was jailed for 18 months, suspended for two years. Pitchfork had told police that he never intended to murder the two girls – merely to achieve a sexual thrill by exposing himself to them.

certain details of his family life. On January 22 1986 Kelly stepped forward at the incident room pretending to be Colin Pitchfork. His blood sample was taken and the name of Colin Pitchfork was removed from suspects in due course when it was found that his DNA did not match that found at the murder scene.

But Kelly, essentially a decent young man who was cajoled and pressurised into taking the test, began to have his doubts. He talked it over among workmates who also thought that Pitchfork's reluctance might be based on more than a mere suspicion that the police were after him for previous convictions of exposing himself.

One of these workmates went to police and told them of the deception. A police squad swooped that night and both men were arrested. As he was being taken into custody it dawned on police that only Pitchfork and one other man, excused from giving a sample for medical reasons, were the only ones who did not respond to their appeal for help. And when a sample of Pitchfork's blood and hair was sent off for analysis it linked him to both murders, murders which he could no longer deny.

He appeared at Leicester Crown Court a year later where he was sentenced to two terms of life imprisonment and concurrent terms for the sexual assaults on the girls, plus conspiracy to pervert the course of justice. Mr. Brian Escott-Cox, QC, prosecuting, told the court that he had gone to

Both were random attacks that went wrong. He became highly aroused, raped them then killed them to prevent identification.

After Pitchfork's conviction, the potential for genetic fingerprinting leaped onwards. Police may soon have genetic "photofits" at their disposal, predicting the sex, race, hair and eye colour of suspects from forensic samples. Dr. Jeffreys said that rapid advances in molecular genetics means that semen, blood or even tiny traces of saliva from the scene of a crime could reveal their owner's characteristics. DNA profiles are anonymous at present – it is impossible to tell if samples are from a teenager or a 50-year-old.

AN IMPERFECT SOLUTION

But Dr. Jeffreys said that "decoding" a person's genetic make-up would lead to even more clues. He said: "Criminal investigations where DNA evidence is available will frequently flounder due to the lack of a suspect. The sex of an individual can already be determined by a simple method of DNA analysis, but that is about it.

"Some of the difficulties scientists face include height, which is partly due to genetic make-up but also partly due to environment. It's not as simple as saying: 'Here's a band on the DNA fingerprint so their nose will be a certain number of centimetres long.' There might be a case for keeping the profiles of previous offenders. In the end it will come down to assessing whether such a database would be cost effective." Soon, very soon, what Dr. Jeffreys calls "fantastically small" amounts of DNA could lead to full genetic profiles. It means a kidnapper who licks the stamp for his ransom demand could be caught by the minute spittle left on it. Such is the power of the discovery that Dr. Jeffreys stumbled on by accident!

Now both the Home Office and the FBI in America are considering a DNA database that would span both countries. A database of all previous sex offenders – given that a high proportion of them re-offend after release from jail – might be the logical course to pursue. Dr. Jeffreys makes the point that had there been one in effect when Pitchfork was around, "we would have caught him, the Yorkshire Ripper and every rapist and murderer when there is

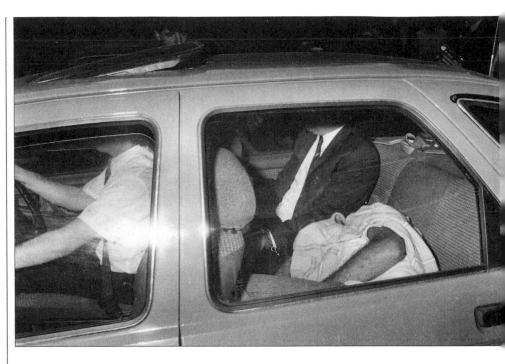

Above: *Colin Pitchfork, his head hidden under a blanket, is driven away from a court hearing. He was eventually sentenced to life.*

Opposite Top: *Yorkshire Ripper, Peter Sutcliffe (extreme right), might have been caught more quickly if DNA had been in existence when he was on the loose in the 1970s.*

Opposite Below: *A smiling killer in a morning suit – Colin Pitchfork on his wedding day in 1981.*

GIVEN THE POTENTIAL OF DNA TESTING, THE ONLY CRUCIAL QUESTION IS HOW FAR HUMAN CURIOSITY WISHES TO GO

---

plenty of biological evidence but no suspect". The civil liberties arguments against such a database appear groundless when it is considered that the genetic code reveals absolutely nothing about a person.

"There is no way a bureaucrat could divine anything about you other than the fact that the material came from you – the anonymous nature of these patterns is vital," said Dr. Jeffreys.

Since the success in the murders case the number of applications for DNA tests have multiplied; in the first 18 months following the case he was besieged by immigrant families imploring him to DNA-test their families to establish relationship. "Settling immigration cases has been wonderful," said the professor. "It is wonderfully worthwhile." It has also been used to determine paternity of a baby in a number of lawsuits, which, he says, "just reveal what squalid and complicated lives some people have".

Given the untold potential of the testing, the only crucial question is how far human curiosity wishes to go. Tests can determine if a person is carrying a defective gene which at 20 could lead to the onset of a fatal disease at 40 or 50. "Do people really want to know about these time bombs inside them?" he asked.

Yet whatever the future applications, Leicestershire police and the people of that county have cause to be eternally grateful to him for putting behind bars a man who deserved no place in decent society.

SILENT WITNESSES
The Maggot Murder

A bleached skull and some rotting bones… nothing to give a clue to detectives with regard to who might have killed the victim whose gravesite they were now gathered around. But an honest army of silent witnesses, in the shape of loathsome, writhing maggots, would finally capture the killer.

A pathologist must have a strong stomach as well as steady nerves when it comes to carrying out his or her extraordinary duties. Corpses are rarely in a pristine state – decomposition makes them stink to high-heaven, as well as providing a feeding ground for insects of every kind. This very "unpleasantness" is used now in certain crime-prevention programmes in America. In Columbus, Georgia, for example, first-time drug offenders have to sit through full-blown criminal autopsies. Many of them can cope with the dissection of the body – the removal of the heart, liver, brain for examination – but those who faint invariably do so because of the stench of decomposition, or at the sight of creepy-crawlies that have wormed their way into the cadaver.

But to trained experts these parasites seeking food and refuge in a corpse are sometimes a welcome sight. Their very presence can render up a wealth of clues as

TO TRAINED EXPERTS, PARASITES SEEKING FOOD AND REFUGE IN A CORPSE ARE SOMETIMES A WELCOME SIGHT

Opposite: *Maggots feasting on a human skull.*

Below: *Police search Bracknell Woods for clues to the corpse in The Maggot Murder.*

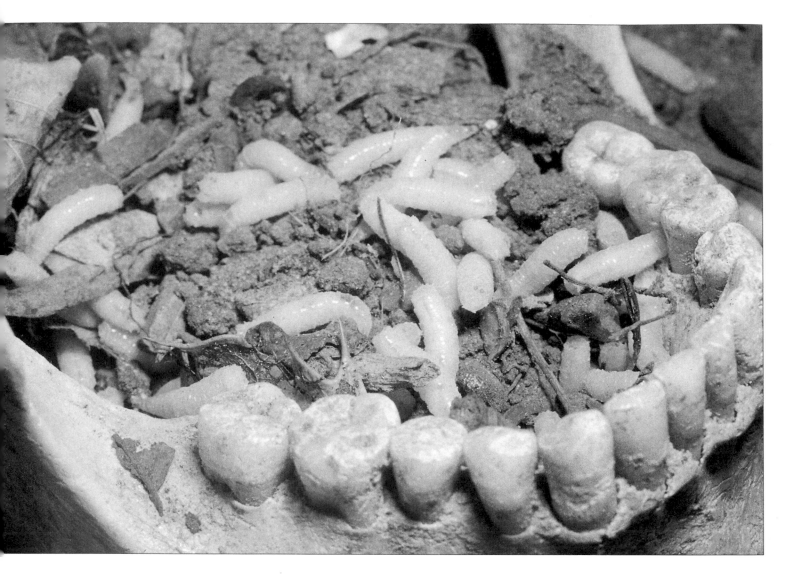

Above: *Maggots writhe between the teeth of the victim's skull. They would hold the key to solving the otherwise baffling case.*

THOSE WRIGGLING, WHITE, FAT BODIES LIVING WITHIN THE CORPSE WOULD PROVIDE THE KEY TO THE KILLER

to when the person died, how long they had been exposed to air before death and even provide clues as to where the murder may have taken place. In June 1964 Britain's foremost Home Office pathologist Professor Keith Simpson began his examination of a maggot-infested corpse. The stench was terrible, the state of the body lamentable. But never was an expert more glad to see those wriggling, white, fat bodies living within the corpse... visitors who would provide the key to the killer.

Two 13-year-old boys out for a day's fishing near Bracknell Woods in Berkshire on June 28 of that year paused before going to the riverbank to look for a small, dead animal that might be maggot-infested. Paul Fay and Tony King had done this countless times before, seeking out a pigeon or a rabbit, maybe a starling, that had been long dead and ripe for larvae. As they cut through the dry undergrowth they saw an unusual sight – maggots writhing on a

mound of grass when usually they had to sweep aside leaves or undergrowth to get to the object which they fed off.

It was quite a find and would save the boys plenty of time in their quest for live bait. Yet as they started to collect the maggots, they pulled away the turf to reveal a semi-rotted human arm with a hand still attached to it that suddenly flopped out of the hole. Running out of fear and shock the boys bolted to the nearest police station. Their fishing trip abandoned, the maggot site became a murder investigation within 30 minutes.

Detective Chief Superintendent Arthur Lawson was disturbed at his home shortly after his Sunday lunch that day. The chief of the Berkshire CID, he supervised the careful removal of the corpse from its shallow grave. The body was that of a fully-grown man, fully clothed, lying on his back, the head wrapped in towelling. Scenes-of-crime officers – SOCOS in police parlance – were unable to garner much evidence from the actual gravesite. There were no tyre tracks visible through the vegetation on the soft earth to indicate how the body was brought there; no weapons, glasses or other pieces of clothing that might have belonged to the unfortunate victim's murderer were found either.

Lawson speculated from the state of the body that it might have been several weeks old, but Professor Simpson – who had also been disturbed from a post-lunch snooze in his garden – surprised him by deducing that the body was no more than 12 days old at the most. "It is astonishing how quickly maggots will eat up the flesh," he said. "I have seen a body reduced to this state in as little as ten days."

THE EXPERT'S VIEW

It became clear that the forensic evidence offered up by the cadaver would be of supreme importance – both in identification and in any prosection of the perpetrator of the crime. Professor Simpson described the maggots in his autobiography *Forty Years of Murder*.

"I thought it safe to assume the maggots were larvae of the bluebottle Calliphora erythocephalus, but I preserved samples because the maggots of other flies of the calliphorine type, with slightly different hatching times, are not dissimilar to the naked eye. The ordinary life history of the bluebottle is quite simple: the eggs are laid in daylight, usually sunlight, and in warm weather they hatch on the first day.

"The tiny 'first instar' maggot sheds its skin after eight to 14 hours, and the second instar after a further two to three days. The third instar, the fisherman's maggot, feeds voraciously for five or six days before going into a pupa case. The larvae I was looking at were mature, indeed elderly, fat, indolent, third-stage maggots, but they were not in pupa cases. Therefore I estimated that the eggs had been laid nine or ten days earlier. Adding a little more time to allow for the bluebottles getting to the dead body, I reckon death had occurred on the 16th or the 17th of June.' The maggots were to play a vital role in the case.

Due to the extreme fragility of the corpse, Professor Simpson decided to do some of his autopsy at the site, fearing that the body might break up in transit. Tell-tale small pools of blood either side of the head and a similar pool inside the voice box – coupled with the detection of crushed bones in the larynx – told him that the man had died with a vicious blow to the windpipe, perhaps more than one.

Back in the laboratory the remains yielded other data: he had broken his left arm when he was young and the fracture had not set properly and the skeleton measured 5ft 3ins. Now it was a question of matching the remains to a person – which was where Professor Simpson left off and the police came into their own again.

Below: *The decomposing body of Peter Thomas, a man who found justice through the maggots which feasted on his remains.*

As with all murders the immediate checks are with missing persons. Chief Supt. Lawson checked with the central office for such information – then, as now, Scotland Yard. The missing persons bureau highlighted the fact that a Peter Thomas had vanished from his home in Lydney, Gloucestershire, on June 16.

A Scotland Yard "heavyweight" detective, Superintendent Horace Faber, had been down to the countryside at the request of the local constabulary to help out on the disappearance. When he learned that there might be a link between the missing person and the corpse that had turned up in the woods 100 miles away he attached himself to the crime squad.

Thomas matched the characteristics of the corpse. He was listed as being the same height as the cadaver, he had broken his left arm in childhood and, more importantly, he had a criminal record. Simpson was telegraphed to take fingerprints off of the decaying flesh of the corpse. They established beyond doubt that the corpse which had become a feast for maggots was indeed that of the man from Lydney. The police now had identity and cause of death – it

Above: *The bluebottle fly, whose larvae hatched on the body of Thomas, thereby providing the forensic expert with invaluable clues as to his death.*

Opposite Top: *Dr Keith Simpson, the undisputed genius of British forensic science. His expertise would crack the mystery of The Maggot Murder.*

Opposite Bottom: *Dr Simpson in his usual pose, crouching down at a crime scene – this one is the infamous Haigh 'acid bath' murders.*

was time to concentrate on the killer and the motive for the violent end.

Enquiries soon discovered that Thomas had been living a life on the edge of poverty in a wooden bungalow. The scene at his home was one of bachelor untidiness writ large – half-eaten meals, uncleaned plates, empty soup tins everywhere. He was receiving unemployment benefit, although a police search of the unkempt property revealed that, some years earlier, he had been in receipt of the not-insubstantial sum of £5,000 in an inheritance, left to him by his father in his will when he died three years earlier. The money was loaned to a Thomas Brittle, a heating-radiator salesman of Hook, Hampshire.

More significantly, paperwork revealed that "this debt shall be repaid no later than the 30th of June 1964". The instinct of hardened policemen was aroused by the coincidence that the due date of the loan repayment fell in the same month that the man was murdered. Suspicion fell upon the Thomas Brittle to whom the money had been loaned – loaned, it later turned out, against the advice of Thomas' lawyer who said it was a "bad prospect".

Detectives learned that Brittle had advertised in a newspaper seeking investors for an agricultural project – namely that he would pay 12-and-a-half per-cent for six months to anyone willing to offer up the cash. Thomas did – and it was to cost him his life. Brittle was questioned, cautioned, and arrested for the murder – despite the lack of evidence against him.

LIES AND ALIBIS

In custody he admitted that he had gone to Lydney on June 16 – the day of the dead man's disappearance. He said that he had repaid the money – although, of course, it was not to be found in Thomas' modest bungalow, nor at the crime scene. He said he had won the repayment cash on the horses at Epsom, although could not give to police the names of the winning steeds. There was no forensic on his clothes, on his car or on any of his possessions to link him to the murder. And he produced a hitch-hiker to swear that he had picked him up en route to pay back the money. "I ask you, would I have given a lift to someone if I was on my way to kill him?" he asked police with a look of wide-eyed innocence.

Police had expected to find at least a trace of evidence in the car. Crimes of violence are always about an exchange

between parties, whether of bodily fluids, blood or tissue. The criminal and the victim tend to leave traces – however microscopic – of their presence. Yet on Thomas' body there was nothing connected to Brittle. The case dragged on for months – then there came a break. A Dennis Roberts, who lived in Gloucester, stepped forward to say he had seen Thomas at Gloucester bus station on June 20 – a date he was certain of because he was on strike for the first time in his life from the fabrics factory where he worked. This information seemed to clear Brittle – he had the testimony of the hitch-hiker to back him up that he had been going to see him four days previously. If he was still alive four days later, how could he be the culprit?

In the end, it came down to the workings of the maggots – those silent but ravenous guardians of the corpse – which would determine guilt or innocence.

Professor Simpson was working in his laboratory when Faber of the Yard came to see him about the testimony of Roberts. "Is it possible he was killed on the 20th and was only dead for eight days?" Faber asked Simpson. "No it isn't," answered the expert. "And I am ready to stand up to severe cross-examination on the point if it comes to trial."

To back up his verbal assurance Professor Simpson attached a note to the Director of Public Prosecutions, on whom the decision rested as to whether to bring Brittle to trial. It read: "I have today been shown a copy of a statement by Dennis John Roberts to the effect that on Saturday, 20th June, he saw a man whom he recognised as Peter Thomas at a bus station.

"The condition of the body when examined in the wood suggested in the first instance, while still at the scene – 'some nine or ten days, possibly more' – was a minimum period. Nothing in the post-mortem state of the body suggested any special conditions likely to have accelerated the ordinary process of maggot infestation and disintegration of the body. I have had considerable experience in the timing of death and would regard Dennis Roberts' statement as being wholly inconsistent with my findings." Professor Simpson was prepared to swear on the writhing larvae of the bluebottle fly against the word of a defence witness.

The DPP passed on the prosecution – he felt there was not enough evidence to convict Brittle. However, a jury at the inquest returned an extraordinary verdict – "that Thomas had been murdered by a person around about the 17th of June". And in a rider they named that person as Brittle. The Coroner then had no choice but to commit Brittle into custody while a reluctant DPP pressed ahead with his prosecution – a prosecution in which he hoped writhing maggots would make the star witnesses!

The counsel for the defence in the case was the redoubtable Quintin Hogg, later to become Lord Hailsham, the Lord Chancellor. Professor Simpson knew he

to hatch, and the three stages of maggot instar to develop before pupation.

I added up the times and in court said, as deliberately and as purposefully as I knew how: 'I had no doubt that this man had been dead some ten days.' Nine or ten was a minimum." He also supplied expert testimony on the blow or blows which killed the dead man – in his opinion karate-chop type strikes to the throat, such as might be administered by someone who was an expert in unarmed combat. And the defendant, it turned out, had taken Commando training in the British Army and had learned such manoeuvres…

Professor Simpson was too much of an expert to doubt – even for Quintin Hogg, who asked no further questions of him. He tried to shake the prosecution evidence about the maggots from Professor McKenny-Hughes, a specialist in insects. He hoped this eminent entomologist would be able to refute the testimony about the maggots, but he only reinforced the pathologist's opinion. When asked if the flies might have been laying their eggs at midnight rather than midday the academic replied: "Oh dear me no. No self-respecting bluebottle lays eggs at midnight. At midday, perhaps, but not at midnight."

The trial took place nine months after Brittle was arrested. The prosecution made much of the fact that time had blurred the memory of the man who had allegedly seen the dead man at the bus stop. But Dennis Roberts was not to be dissauded from his initial testimony and the jury, after a five day trial, had to decide upon the unreliable sighting or the expert testimony of Professor Simpson. They decided the maggots were more reliable and Brittle was given a life sentence for murder.

Professor Simpson said: "The case was particularly satisfying to me. My insistence on the timing of death has become pretty well known, to the police, to the Director of Public Prosecutions, the lawyers – and the Press, who would have scented a public disgrace for me if I had been wrong."

Legal expert James Staniford added this postscript: "It was an extraordinary victory for forensic expertise, indeed a landmark case, presented in such a way so as not to baffle the jury and allow them to come to the right conclusion about a particularly cold-blooded murderer."

would be given a hard time in the witness box by this courtroom expert, but he was convinced that the maggots had to have been there before the time Roberts swore he saw the victim alive at the bus station.

CLEAR EVIDENCE

In his autobiography he recounted: "When I was examined by the crown counsel, Ralph Cusack, I set out as clearly and as briefly as I could the nature of the fat, third instar maggot, not yet pupated, yet plainly having passed the growing-up stages from the day the eggs hatched. I further set out the several periods of time that it took eggs

Above: *The counsel for the defence in the case was the redoubtable Quintin Hogg, later to become Lord Hailsham, the Lord Chancellor.*

GORDON HAY
Marks of Death

From the horrifying condition of her dead body, it was obvious that 15-year-old schoolgirl Linda Peacock had fallen prey to a savage beast. There were few clues left at the murder scene to aid police… but, thanks to teethmarks that had been left on the corpse, justice was eventually done.

They found the girl in a cemetery, her violated body lying between two graves and beneath the shadow of a fully grown yew tree. The little town of Biggar, midway between Edinburgh and Glasgow, was not used to such depraved murder. The girl, later identified as 15-year-old Linda Peacock, had not been raped during the frenzied assault on her on the night of August 6 1967, but her clothing was pushed up to expose her breasts. When police were called to the murder scene the next morning they began the usual hunt for clues – the search for minutiae which even the cleverest criminal must leave behind at the site of a crime.

There was little to make the scene of crime officer and the pathologist happy about the possibility of finding who had done this to the poor victim. But then a veteran police sergeant noticed the strange bruising around the right breast and took photographs of it. Detective Sgt. John Paton had attended dozens of murder scenes, arsons, rapes and break-ins during his 20 years on the force. There was something about the bruising which made him convinced that it was a human bite, although it did not have the usual teeth outline. It was he alone who had grasped the significance of the wound – and a good job he did. For in doing so the case of Linda Peacock went into the criminal history books because her killer was the first ever to be caught by his teeth.

Criminal odontology – the study of teeth in relation to crimes and criminals – was a relatively murky area to British experts in the 1950s. The Scandinavians seemed to lead the world in research and the application of the new science in relation to crime solving. Teeth, it was learned, largely thanks to the expertise of Swedish expert Gosta Gustavson – have many of the properties of fingerprints when it comes to individual characteristics. Together with his wife Anna Greta he had also discovered it was possible to divine the age of a corpse by careful microscopic investigation of molars. Yet there had never been a conviction in a British court based solely on teeth identification the way there had been with

Opposite: *Linda Peacock's body, covered by tarpaulin in the graveyard where it was discovered.*

Below: *Bitemarks would lead to the killer of innocent schoolgirl Linda.*

Above: *Police at the Peacock murder scene undertaking the usual hunt for clues. But clues were in short supply in this case.*

WHEN LINDA PEACOCK'S BITEMARKS WERE ANALYSED FURTHER IT SET IN MOTION A BRILLIANT CRIMINAL INVESTIGATION

Right: *Twenty years before the Hay case, a vampire killer had spread terror across London, claiming five victims.*

fingerprints and blood groups. When Linda Peacock's bitemarks were analysed further it set in motion a brilliant criminal investigation which would change that.

Dr. Warren Harvey, Scotland's leading expert in forensic odontology and lecturer to the Scottish Detective Training School, was the first to inspect Sgt. Paton's photographs. He concurred that the marks on her breast were indeed of teeth and human ones at that. Yet there was a troublesome aspect to their location; it seemed from examination of the corpse – she had been strangled and the bite was inflicted just moments after death – that the bite had come from behind. It would have taken an act of some considerable contortion, but was not impossible. The only formidable task was finding a man whose teeth matched the indentations of the bite.

INITIAL SUSPICIONS

Chief Superintendent William Muncie of the Lanarkshire CID handled the police investigation while Dr. Harvey enlisted specialist help from further afield. The crime bore all the classic hallmarks of an attempted sexual assault that had gone wrong. He believed that the girl had been approached for sex, she had resisted and in doing so had sealed her fate. Such crimes are in the category of "opportunist" and are rarely planned; Muncie was certain, therefore, that he was looking for a local man with a knowledge of the area and, obviously, the girl. He and his officers spent ten days interviewing all 3,000 men in the locality and, to a man, they all had alibis and were eliminated from the enquiry.

The only place he hadn't been to was a nearby borstal for young offenders where 29 apprentices-in-crime were undergoing incarceration and training in the hope that they would go straight. Dr. Harvey said to Muncie: "It seems as if your enquiries are now winding down in regards to local males on the outside – perhaps it would be prudent for me to ask you to check the teeth of those inside. I think that dental casts should be made of all the inmates." Each boy inside signed a form which read: "I have been told that this is in relation to the investigation into the death

Below: *Police chiefs William Muncie (left) and Det. Insp. Weir pore over maps of the murder area in their hunt for the killer.*

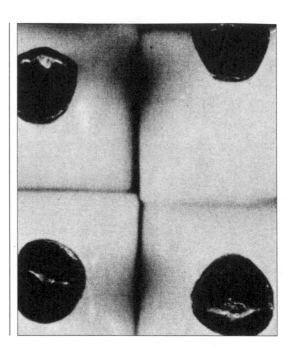

Left: *Professor Keith Simpson, Britain's most eminent criminal pathologist, played a key role in the investigation.*

Right: *Copper plate models of Gordon Hay's teeth, clearly illustrating the pits which would trap him.*

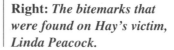

Left: *Casts of Hay's upper and lower teeth, vital links in the chain of evidence that led to him being fingered as the girl's killer.*

of Linda Peacock. It has been made clear to me that I can refuse to comply with the test. It has also been made clear to me that should my dental impressions be linked with other evidence in the case they may be produced as evidence."

The boys in the borstal, aged between 14 and 17 – none of whom possessed a particularly high IQ – all volunteered for the project which, if nothing else, gave them a day out from their drab surroundings. At Glasgow's Dental Hospital, plaster casts were made of each one's teeth. Experiments then began trying to match individual teeth to the marks found on the girl's breast. The largest mark was a very dark oval, about 13mm by 7mm, and there were four smaller ones.

Dr. Harvey later said: "I examined the casts with Detective Inspector Osborne Butler of the Identification Bureau of Glasgow Police. Several were instantly recognisable as being useless to the case because they possessed no jagged teeth capable of inflicting the marks. I decided to call in the aid of another expert."

The expert he called upon was Britain's most eminent criminal pathologist and forensic expert – Professor Keith Simpson – who listed the notorious Haigh acid bath

EXPERIMENTS THEN BEGAN, TRYING TO MATCH INDIVIDUAL TEETH TO THE MARKS FOUND ON THE GIRL'S BREAST

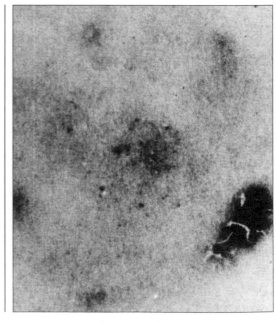

Right: *The bitemarks that were found on Hay's victim, Linda Peacock.*

murders as one of his celebrated cases. Increasingly, Professor Simpson had been at the forefront of advancing the scientific application of forensic odontology into crime solving. He was a great friend of the Swedish expert Gustavson and had given evidence on the importance of teeth and their value as a source of clues at a number of trials and inquests.

At his base in Guys Hospital, London, Professor Simpson and Dr. Harvey made new casts of resin, which were tougher, and whittled the 29 boys down to five major suspects. From the resin casts they made models capable of "occlusal" movements – that is, capable of biting in much the same way as a living human. A female body was brought from the morgue and tests were begun. Initially, Simpson had concurred

Above: *Guys Hospital, London, where expert analysis led to the teeth which belonged to the killer of Linda Peacock.*

LEFT ON THE PROFESSOR'S NAIL WERE MARKS IDENTICAL TO THOSE THAT HAD BEEN FOUND ON THE DEAD GIRL

---

with Harvey that one particular cast labelled No.14 – the experts were not provided with names – was the prime suspect, but tests ruled him out completely. Starting from the beginning again, all 29 casts were examined under the most stringent scientific conditions. Attention focussed on two curiously shaped abrasions – abrasions which no-one believed could have been made by teeth; there was certainly no such mention of them in Gustavson's "Bible" *Forensic Odontology*.

But later, re-examination of the teeth of suspect No.11 turned up something definite. Dr. Harvey pressed the upper and lower right canines of the cast into his thumbnail for several seconds and with considerable pressure; when he released them, left on the base of the nail were

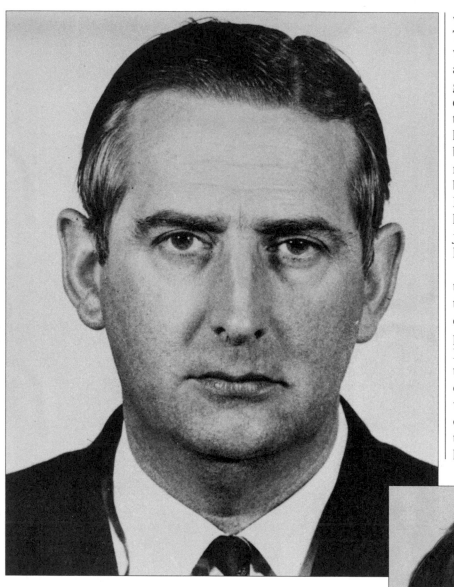

was not so far fetched as it might seem. The mark of the ligature round her neck was most pronounced in the front and least at the back, showing she had been strangled from behind. Blood in front of her left ear, from one of her head wounds, had clotted while she was vertical. Her left wrist had been tied with a piece of string – burned off after death, leaving a scorchmark and a blister – and her arm had probably been held behind her. And, although Harvey and Butler did not yet know it, mud had been observed on the knees of No.11's jeans that night, suggesting he had been kneeling on the ground."

It was five weeks after the murder by the time the final tests had been done and all three members of the scientific team were convinced that Number 11 was their suspect. That coincided with Chf. Supt. Muncie's theories too because he had spent time interviewing the boys and the only one whose alibi he didn't feel comfortable with was his. No. 11 was a callow 17-year-old called Gordon Hay, a hardened petty thief, car stealer and general bad boy who had been in trouble with the law since he

Above: *Det. Supt. Osborne Butler of the identification bureau of the Glasgow police co-operated closely with odontologists on the case.*

Right: *Gordon Hay's teethmarks condemned him as the killer.*

"THE MAN WHO HAD KILLED HER HAD COME OVER THE GIRL'S SHOULDER WHILE SHE WAS SITTING… HE HAD EXTREME DEXTERITY"

marks identical to those that were found on the dead girl.

Harvey was still concerned about the angle at which the bite marks appeared to have been made. Later, in a scientific paper about the case, he wrote: "Since, to put it mildly, this orientation seemed strange a further attempt was made with the other four models. But apart from the already-discredited No.14, none of the others fitted at all. It was my opinion that the attacker, the man who had killed her, had come over the girl's right shoulder while she was sitting and that he had extreme dexterity."

Professor Simpson, writing of the case years later, said: "The medical evidence showed this was nine. He was also a compulsive liar, coupled with a feral cunning which alerted him when danger was around. There were no clues to link him to the murder other than the statement of one other boy and Muncie's own hunch. As far as the authorities were concerned, all the boys were tucked up in their beds in the barrack-style dorms when Linda Peacock met her untimely and violent end.

KEY EVIDENCE

The other lad in the dormitory, who remained anonymous due to his age, told Muncie: "On August 6 one of our masters saw Hay in the dining room at about 10.00pm and another one saw him at 10.30pm lying in bed in his pyjamas. But I saw him come through the window. His hair was blown about and he was dirty and sweaty and out of breath. We had heard some screaming from the direction of the cemetery and I couldn't help thinking that he had had something to do with it. The day before he had been allowed out on a good conduct pass and had gone to a local fair where he met a girl. He couldn't stop bragging about her when he came back – said she was a 'nice bit of stuff' and that he would like to have sex with her."

Above and Left: *Linda Peacock – a life of promise lay ahead until she was brutally murdered by a deranged borstal boy. Linda was a gentle soul who loved animals as much as she loved people.*

Above: *Linda's pretty home, a home from which she went missing forever on that fateful night in 1967.*

> "CIRCUMSTANTIAL EVIDENCE WAS CLEARLY INSUFFICIENT AND, THEREFORE, THE DENTAL EVIDENCE WAS CRUCIAL"

Muncie's detectives interviewed Hay again but kept back from him the evidence of the youth who had seen him come in the window. He even volunteered to them that he had indeed met the dead girl, but that he was sound asleep when she was killed. There was no hard evidence, just circumstantial, to link him to the crime. Police even made a healthy P.C. run from the crime scene to the borstal to see if it could be done in a couple of minutes; it could.

DISMAL RUMOURS

Yet there was consternation among senior officers, shared by the Procurator Fiscal, that a prosecution would fail without more tangible evidence. Professor Simpson said: "Circumstantial evidence was clearly insufficient and, therefore, the dental evidence was crucial. Harvey and Butler came back to London and showed me the latest results of their work. I encouraged them to make a more detailed study of Hay's teeth and to prepare scaled 'overlay' transparencies. They fitted the scale bitemark print perfectly – of that there was no doubt."

Dr. Harvey researched deeper and found that minute pits on Hay's teeth could have been caused by drinking water without fluoride added when he was a child. This was significant because in previous criminal cases abroad, bitemark identifications had usually required the identification of five teeth – the team had identified just two. But an examination of government records in Scotland showed that no-one else had more than one pitted-tooth. Professor Simpson felt that all the evidence of his teeth put together would be enough to gain a conviction, adding: "A jury should have no difficulty in understanding this evidence and appreciating its simple strength. It is akin to tool-marking evidence or fingerprints."

The Procurator Fiscal decided to let the prosecution proceed. Hay was arrested and charged with murder and pleaded not guilty when he came before Lord Justice Grant at the High Court of Justice in Edinburgh. His trial lasted nine days, during which Hay vehemently denied having anything to do with the crime. The evidence – medical evidence on the teeth alone amounting to 400 pages of manuscript – would have to speak for itself with the aid of testimony from Dr. Harvey and Professor Simpson.

COOL DEFENCE

It was Professor Simpson who would face the cool, challenging questions from Hay's defence counsel William Stewart, Q.C., who attempted to call up the expertise of Gustavson in defending his client – a case of trying to rescue him by using the evidence of those who would seek to damn him. Professor Simpson later wrote in his autobiography: "When I was in the witness box the defence counsel, as I had expected, quoted from the Swedish expert Gustavson's book, to which I had written a foreword published in an English translation. 'Do you agree with the view expressed inside the book'," asked Stewart, "'that at least four or five teeth, and they say they are adjacent teeth, should correspond exactly before a positive identification can be made?'

"'I think it is a sound view,' I answered, 'but I think probably a better attitude is a general one; that is to say that the more points of comparison that can be pointed to, the more points of proof and the fewer the less certain.'"

Hay sat impassive throughout his trial, paying no heed to the massive press attention or the sketch artists who drew him while he was in the dock. He understood that, on the surface, everything rested on those tooth marks and whether or not a jury would accept such evidence to condemn him to imprisonment. The trial lasted nine days and at the end of it observers thought that the accused man had a singularly smug look on his face, as if he expected to be out that evening.

After deliberating less than three hours the jury returned a verdict of guilty. Hay was attempting to shout at the judge when he was hurried to the cells to begin his detention "at Her Majesty's pleasure". Police commented later that friends of Linda had told them of the borstal boy she had met at the fair, but that she had not been attracted to him. Hay, for his part, was inflamed with lust, particularly at the sight of her well-developed breasts. She had resisted him. In his frenzy and with his agile body, he had lunged at her from behind to leave the signature that would commit him to jail for years.

As part of his summing up, Lord Justice Grant paid special praise to the work of the forensic experts. "Forensic odontology," he said, "as it is called, is a relatively new science. But of course there must be a first time for everything."

Because of Hay's insatiable lust, a lassie had died... and a young man who was supposed to be salvaged from crime had gone into the record books.

IN HIS FRENZY HE HAD LUNGED AT HER TO LEAVE THE SIGNATURE THAT WOULD COMMIT HIM TO JAIL FOR YEARS

Below: *William Muncie, Chief Superintendent of the Lanarkshire CID, handled the police investigation. It was of great comfort to him and Linda's family to know that justice had been done.*

EMMETT-DUNNE
A Deadly Affair

Frederick Emmett-Dunne brought shame upon his British Army uniform. He dallied with the wife of another soldier and when his passion was inflamed, killed his rival. It was almost the perfect murder, but forensic science was to unearth the evil sergeant and ensure a long prison sentence for him.

Post-war Germany for British Army garrison troops was a dismal billet. Rationing was still enforced, the local population was often resentful and the bombed-out towns and cities offered little in the way of entertaining diversions. Life, for the most part, centred on the base itself where the wives of married men became as bored as their husbands in the tiresome duty of policing a defeated nation.

The boredom of one such wife, and the interest shown in her by a sergeant named Frederick Emmett-Dunne, was to lead to murder… a murder the sergeant nearly got clean away with. But 15 months after the lid was closed on the coffin of his rival the body still yielded vital clues – clues a second forensic expert would detect… and finally send Emmett-Dunne to jail for life.

It was early in the morning of December 1 1953 that the body of Sgt. Ernie Watters was found hanging in a barrack block at the Glamorgan Barracks in Duisberg, "discovered" by Sgt. Emmett-Dunne and another man. It seemed from the scene that it was a suicide; on the ground was a bucket which had been turned on its side, indicating that the dead man had stood on it as a makeshift gallows and kicked it aside to allow the rope to tighten around his neck.

There was an Army enquiry followed by an Army inquest which judged that the unfortunate sergeant had taken his own life due to depression – even though all who knew him testified that he was a cheerful man with seemingly little to worry about. He had no money problems, no skeletons in his closet and was an efficient and well-liked soldier.

But Dr. Alan Womack, the pathologist who carried out the post-mortem, added his expert testimony to ensure that a suicide verdict was recorded. Dr. Womack testified that death had come from hanging because of the broken cricoid bone – a bone in the throat just below the thyroid – in his neck. He was wrong, and because of it a murderer walked scot-free.

NO SECRETS

Sgt. Emmett-Dunne had killed him, and even before the ink was dry on the inquest report the rumours began circulating about him. Emmett-Dunne had taken a fancy to Watters' German-born wife Mia some time before and his attentions had not been unrequited. There were snatched brief encounters while her husband was on duty and he was not; excursions to the local cinema and picnics in the rolling countryside.

At dances and other social functions the other members of this insular community tut-tutted at the apparent closeness with which they danced, the glances that lingered too long over the mess table. None of this was presented at the inquest, of course, but six months after the body of Sgt. Watters

Above: *Sergeant Reginald Ernie Watters and his German bride Mia. She later found solace in the arms of another sergeant.*

Opposite: *Military police escort Frederick Emmett-Dunne (centre), as he faces charges of murdering a fellow soldier.*

AN ARMY INQUIRY FOLLOWED BY AN ARMY INQUEST JUDGED THAT THE UNFORTUNATE SERGEANT HAD TAKEN HIS OWN LIFE

Above and Below: *The killer and his black widow – Sergeant Emmett-Dunne acts as escort to the former Mrs Mia Watters.*

had been laid to rest Sgt. Emmett-Dunne married the widow. There were stage whispers of "I told you so" sweeping the camp, and soon they were to come to the ears of the top brass.

The Army decided that perhaps the inquest first time around had been too hasty. Anonymous letters were sent to them informing on the marriage between the widow and Emmett-Dunne. After consultations with the War Office and the Home Office, the Army was informed that it had no choice but to call in Scotland Yard.

By the time Dr. Francis Camps, a distinguished Home Office pathologist arrived in Germany accompanied by two detectives from Scotland Yard, Emmett-Dunne and his new bride were back in Britain, the murder now having happened a full 15 months previously.

Of course, what the police needed was evidence of murder – no rumour in the world would stand up to scrutiny in a court of law, be it martial or civilian, without the foundations of truth to underpin it.

FURTHER INVESTIGATIONS

As the body was disinterred in Germany, Emmett–Dunne was questioned at his new home in Somerset, England, about his relationship with Mrs. Watters before she married him. He sensed the direction the conversation was going in and stormed: "My only crime was marrying before the proper lapse of time prescribed by Victorian morality!" Indeed, there was little the police could do without hard evidence – it was his word against a lot of people who smelled something fishy, but could offer nothing by way of hard fact.

The task facing Dr. Camps from the decomposing remains of Watters was to find evidence of murder. Dr. Womack, who had carried out the first post mortem was a skilled and dedicated pathologist, but it turned out that he was mistaken in deciding that the cause of death was strangulation. Dr. Camps laboured intensively in the Army morgue until he came up with the real cause of Watters' demise.

Where the unfortunate man's voice box had been remained evidence of blood. The small bones of the larynx were crushed and he was able to pick them out one by one like small chicken bones. Such bones would not be broken by a rope's pressure but by the sudden, swift, blow of a hand or blunt object. Perhaps, and most probably, surmised the eminent forensic expert, by a man trained in unarmed combat, like a

was still in force in Britain, but not there. He was therefore sentenced to life imprisonment. Immediately after sentencing he was sent back to Britain to serve time in a maximum security jail among other murderers, robbers and rapists. Mia stood by him, claiming she believed in his innocence and that she was certain he had been in a fight that had gone wrong. But there was too much evidence in the trial for her not to be left with some nagging doubts.

FRUITLESS PLEAS

Back home in England he tried his best to get his sentence altered with petitions to the government of the day and even the Queen. All decided that it was best for him to remain behind bars. The case itself is something of a textbook one for criminal pathologists and forensic experts. Crime writer George Crossen said: "If they had been more discreet in their affair the body of the dead man would never have been dug up. If he had not been dug up Dr. Camps would never have detected the clues of the single killing blow.

"If he had not detected the evidence of the single killing blow Emmett-Dunne would have gotten away with that rare thing – the perfect murder. In the end, he was defeated by a medical science that was far, far more precise than him."

We had been good friends who liked to dance together, that is all.

"There is not a word of truth to what the prosecution has had to say."

But he had not reckoned on the damning testimony of a half-brother, Ronald Emmett, who was living in another part of the barracks. He came forward at the last minute to say that the accused had sent for him at 8.00pm on the night of the murder to say that he had killed a man in an argument. He wanted Emmett to give him an alibi, to say that they had been together all evening. He then led his half-brother over to the entrance to the barrack block where he showed him the corpse of Sgt. Watters hidden under a cape. "He said if we could lift him up," said Ronald Emmett in court, "we could make it look like suicide.

"I refused. I went to bed, but I didn't tell anybody, not until now." Ronald Emmett said he had come forward because of the expertise of the Home Office pathologist. "Once he said that it was a blow to throat," he said, "and not some kind of accident, like the fellow had hit his head like I was led to believe, then I felt I had no choice but to speak up." Emmett-Dunne was indeed back home living in Cheshire when the story of the exhumation and discovery was carried out. He added: "In view of the way events moved I knew I had to come forward with the whole story."

The Army tribunal found Frederick Emmett-Dunne guilty in Germany – which was just as well for him. The death penalty

Above and Below: *Scenes outside the court martial in Dusseldorf where Emmett-Dunne was found guilty of murder.*

GEORGI MARKOV
Murder by Umbrella

Bulgarian writer Georgi Markov's sensitivites could not cope with the brutal Bulgarian regime he and his countrymen had to endure under communism. He escaped to Britain, to voice his protests to greater effect. But his life was to end in one of the modern era's most notorious assassinations.

Georgi Markov's murder in London is probably the most intriguing and original assassination of this century. Individuals have certainly been killed in numerous and monstrous ways down the years of this turbulent century – shot, stabbed, garroted, hanged, drowned and poisoned – but none reached the heights of Ian Fleming-esque originality and cunning as the fate which befell Bulgarian defector Markov. He was poisoned as he walked down a London street in broad daylight, his fate sealed by a small poisoned capsule delivered into his leg by – an umbrella! The story of his diabolical end is one that continues to fascinate and mesmerise, long after the communist chieftans who plotted his end have themselves passed into history.

A STRIDENT VOICE

Markov, 49 when he died, was a dissident from the orthodox communist regime in Bulgaria who had managed to defect to the West and settle in London. An educated, urbane individual, he had first angered the totalitarian rulers of his homeland in the late 1960s when he still lived there. Before then, he had towed the party line, written the saccharine-sweet prose that praised the glories of communism.

For his efforts he was rewarded with a BMW car, an opulent home and an account with foreign currency that allowed him to buy the best in luxuries that his countrymen could only dream of. Yet Markov was a sensitive, caring individual who eventually woke up to the blind injustices of the regime and decided to take a stand against them. Then he penned a play about a plot to

Opposite: *Georgi Markov, victim of one of the most cunning assassinations of the Cold War.*

NO ASSASSINATION REACHED THE HEIGHTS OF IAN FLEMING-ESQUE ORIGINALITY AS THAT WHICH BEFELL MARKOV

HE WAS A SENSITIVE, CARING INDIVIDUAL WHO EVENTUALLY WOKE UP TO THE BLIND INJUSTICES OF THE REGIME

Below: *London, where Markov began a new life in the early 1970s.*

murder a general – a work clearly anti-government and perceived by the dictator-in-residence, Todor Zhivkov, as an incitement to civil unrest.

VICIOUS PERSECUTION

Markov suffered the usual state harassment – loss of privileges, surveillance, warnings – before he escaped to Italy and from there to London, where he was granted political asylum. But if Zhivkov and his minions thought they had heard the last of him they were very much mistaken. Markov got a job with the Bulgarian section of the BBC foreign service. From his office at Bush House in the Aldwych, he transmitted messages back to his enslaved homeland that riled the communist chieftains even more. Soon Markov became the magnificent obsession for Zhivkov, who was determined to silence him... one way or another.

On the morning of September 7 1978, Markov drove from his home in Clapham to

MARKOV BECAME THE MAGNIFICENT OBSESSION OF ZHIVKOV WHO WAS DETERMINED TO SILENCE HIM... ONE WAY OR ANOTHER

Below: *Bush House, where Georgi Markov found employment with the BBC in the 1970s.*

Bush House, but the London traffic was appalling. Markov could not get his car parked anywhere near his office and so ended up putting it in a vacant spot near Waterloo Bridge. He walked to his office, completed a day's work and went back around 6.00pm to retrieve his vehicle to move it nearer to Bush House. After parking it near the Strand he once more set off back towards his office when he felt a sharp stab of pain in the back of his right thigh. He thought it had come from the accidental prod of an umbrella, the wielder of the offending instrument being a man in a bus queue. When Markov turned to face the man he mumbled profuse apologies in a thick, Eastern European accent, and then slipped out of the bus queue to jump into a cab.

Just four days later Georgi Markov would be dead.

Upon getting back to the office his leg had already begun to stiffen up. He showed a colleague what had happened and said: "Look at that! Some fool stabbed me with

an umbrella!" He showed off a wound like a pimple, with purple and red widening out from the centre to the flesh around. But Markov had been mistaken in believing he had been stabbed by the umbrella tip itself. In fact, the brolly contained a highly sophisticated spring-loaded device in the tip which actually shot poison into his leg, like a silent dart gun. Markov stayed on at the BBC to read news and current affairs bulletins at 11.00pm, but he felt increasingly feverish – a condition he put down to flu. But he was too ill to work the following day and his wife Annabella drove him to St. James Hospital in Balham when his temperature soared over 100 degrees.

A STRANGE INJURY

Doctors were puzzled by the puncture wound on his thigh – too big to have come from either a hypodermic syringe or an insect bite – but they did not at first perceive its true significance. His condition continued to worsen as the hours wore on. By the third day he was given massive antibiotic injections to try to counter an alarming rise in the white corpuscle count in his bloodstream. Doctors who registered his white corpuscle count upon entry to the hospital listed it as 10,600. Soon it raced to an "unbelievable" 26,300. But Markov still failed to respond to treatment and on the fourth day he died of a massive heart attack.

It was only because of the suddenness and mysteriousness of his death that a postmortem was needed to determine what had actually killed him. When traces of the poison ricin were discovered the telephones rang in Whitehall's corridors of power. Forensic scientist Dr. Robert Keeley found the tiny metal ball in Markov's leg which had been used to deliver the poison while Dr. David Gaul, of the top secret Chemical Defence Establishment at Porton Down, provided all the information on poisons and antidotes. Scotland Yard's Anti-Terrorist Squad and MI5 were also informed of the findings of the autopsy.

Dr. Keeley found the tiny metal ball only after X-rays had been taken around the area of the puncture wound on the deaceased's right thigh. It measured 1.52mm in diameter and was made from an alloy of platinum and iridium, a compound noted for its resistance to corrosion and one which can

Above: *President Zhivkov, Bulgarian ruler at the time of the markov killing.*

THE BROLLY CONTAINED A HIGHLY SOPHISTICATED SPRING-LOADED DEVICE IN THE TIP WHICH ACTUALLY SHOT POISON INTO HIS LEG

only be worked in a high-temperature furnace. The minute sphere was drilled through with two holes that met in a centre well where the poison rested. Dr. Keeley had examined a similar ball sent from Paris once the European intelligence agencies of NATO began co-operating over the disturbing death of Markov. This ball too had been recovered from the body of a Bulgarian defector, Vladimir Kostov, but he had been lucky enough to survive the experience.

A RECIPE FOR DEATH

Dr. Gaul later testified at Markov's inquest in London in January 1979 about the ricin poison. Dr. Gaul said: "Tests have ruled out that he died from any other kind of venom, be it from snakes, scorpions, spiders or marine life. Ricin tests were carried out on a live pig and the symptoms it developed before death were almost identical to those suffered by Mr. Markov before his death."

The ricin poison, he told the inquest, came from the seeds of the castor oil plant which, incidentally, grows in abundance in Bulgaria. "There is no legitimate use for ricin," said Dr. Gaul. "And there is no known antidote."

Mrs. Markov said at the inquest that it was her strong belief that her husband had died at the hands of a foreign assassin

Right: *The assassin's "umberella" contained a sophisticated weapon which was used to inject the poison.*

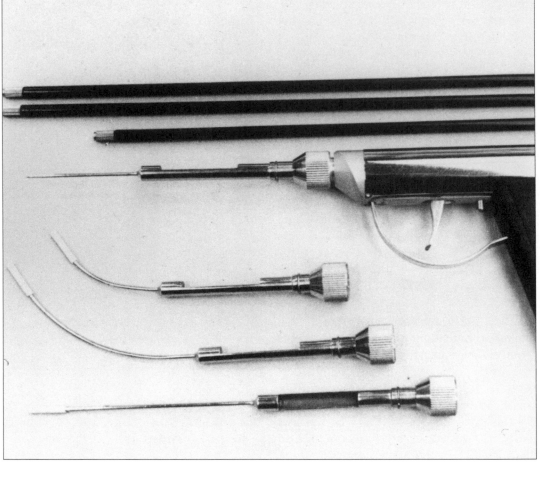

IT STOKED UP THE OLD FEARS OF THE SOVIET COLOSSUS WAITING BEYOND THE HORIZON TO CRUSH ALL OPPONENTS

WHEN THE TRUTH DID COME OUT IT WAS EVERY BIT AS FANTASTIC AS THE THEORIES WOVEN AT THE TIME

working on the orders of the Bulgarian secret police. But Cold War or not, diplomatic niceties had to be maintained. Besides, the operation had been so swift and so well carried out that there was nothing to connect the government of a sovereign country with the murder of a single defector. Whatever Whitehall and MI5 spy-catchers privately thought, in public there was little that could be said or done and, consequently, Markov was recorded by West London Coroner Dr. Gavin Thurston as having been "unlawfully killed".

The papers, however, had a field day. No-one could recall such an audacious murder of an exile in a Western capital. It stoked up the old fears of the Soviet collossus waiting beyond the horizon to crush all opponents and provided endless fodder for polticians, spy writers and right-wingers who spoke menacingly of the Soviet bear waiting to devour us all. Yet it would be many years before the real truth of what happened to Georgi Markov was made public. It would take the collapse of communism in Russia and her satellite states itself. But when the truth did come out it was every bit as fantas-

tic as the theories woven at the time. The mission to eliminate Markov was sanctioned by the head of the KGB himself in Moscow after a request from the paranoid dictator Zhivkov and involved tests on animals and a condemned man.

Details of the assassination were finally revealed by Oleg Kalugin, a Major General in the KGB who was given the task of preparing it by the KGB chairman Yuri Andropov himself. Kalugin, once head of the KGB's counter intelligence branch, was a devoted disciple of the Soviet state. He says he found the task onerous, but that duty meant it was Markov's life... or his.

PRESIDENTIAL HATRED

Kalugin said: "The problem with Markov was raised by the Bulgarians in 1977. Members of their security organisation visited Moscow and told us they had difficulties. Markov was greatly disliked by the Bulgarian president Zhivkov. The president wanted to get rid of him because he was upset by Markov's broadcasts on the BBC's foreign service. They were vehemently anti-communist and anti-Zhivkov. The president felt that Markov's activities were undermining the very foundations of his regime.

"My counterpart in Bulgaria was Vladid Todorov, who regularly came to Moscow to discuss many problems, but he would always end up touching on Markov. At that stage we just listened politely and he went away. But then one day in the spring of 1978 I attended one of our regular meetings with the KGB chairman Yuri Andropov in his office in Moscow. Also there was Vladimir Kyryuchkov, then chief of the intelligence service and later the boss of the KGB, and Vice Admiral Usatov, another senior intelligence official. As the meeting was about to end Kryuchkov said on his own initiative: "We have a request from the Bulgarian interior minister Stoyanov to physically eliminate one of their dissidents, a Mr. Markov. They want us to help them."

A STUNNING REQUEST

"I recall vividly that Andropov was somewhat taken aback. He did not answer straight away. He sat pensively for a while, then he got up and started walking up and down. Then he said: 'You know what? I am against political assassinations. This is not the way to solve our political problems. Let the Bulgarians do it themselves if they wish to. Why should we be involved?' Still walking up and down he ended emphatically: 'I am against it.'

"Kryuchkov, clearly surprised by this negative answer, started cajoling the chairman. 'Mr. Andropov, it is Mr. Zhivkov's request. If we decline to co-operate with the Bulgarians then Mr. Zhivkov might think the Bulgarians are out of favour with the KGB or maybe Mr. Zhivkov is out of favour with the Soviet leadership.

"It is a political problem and we must face it. We cannot simply turn down the Bulgarians' request.'

"Comrade Andropov, who later became president of the USSR, continued walking up and down saying: 'I'm against it.' But he was obviously convinced by the political expediency, and finally he said: 'OK, OK, but I want no direct participation. You provide the weapons, whatever is needed, and give the Bulgarians all the instructions. But then to hell with them. Let them do the final

Left: Yuri Andropov, head of the KGB, gave the order for Markov's assassination to go ahead.

THE PRESIDENT FELT THAT MARKOV WAS UNDERMINING THE VERY FOUNDATIONS OF THE REGIME

job themselves.' Since I was present and my role covered dealing with the problems of primarily Soviet traitors I was called on to handle this, even though a Bulgarian was involved. I was given the job of preparing the ground for the execution of the man.

Below: Dr Bernard Riley arrives to give evidence at the inquest into the defector's death.

Right: *The dissident's proud widow Annabella has tears still glistening in her eyes as she arrives to give evidence at the inquest into his death.*

THREE TYPES OF POISON, AND THE MEANS OF DELIVERING IT INTO MARKOV'S BODY, WERE DISCUSSED

"IT PROPELLED A SMALL PELLET FILLED WITH POISON WHICH PENETRATED THE SKIN AND DISSOLVED QUICKLY"

Chairman Andropov told me: 'Kalugin, you take charge of this. You do it.'"

Kalugin summoned Colonel Sergei Golobev, who ran "wet" operations for the KGB – wet being the in-house term for assassinations – and told him to report to the agency's Directorate of Science and Technology which dealt with everything from wiretaps to chemical weapons. Three types of poison, and the means of delivering it into Markov's body, were discussed before it was settled that the umbrella would be used.

He went on: "The Bulgarians had designed a small gadget like a fountain pen, about five inches long, which could be fired from a distance of a metre and-a-half.

It propelled a small pellet filled with poison which penetrated the skin and dissolved quickly, leaving no trace. The device was fitted into an umbrella and operated from the handle. But the Bulgarians, wary of earlier failures and the fury of Zhivkov, insisted on testing it first. They tested it on a horse and the horse died within hours. They then tested it on a man who was under sentence of death."

AN INHUMAN TEST

"The man was taken out of his condemned cell for a walk and the guards shot at him with this pellet from the distance of about a metre. The man was startled as he felt the pain in the back of his knee, and started shouting and crying. He thought the moment of execution had arrived without anyone telling him. Then he calmed down, recovered and actually survived the attack. Moscow was informed and the scientists started working again to try to enhance the poison. In the end they came up with more effective pellets.

"After Markov was executed I was given a small token of the Bulgarians' appreciation – a Browning hunting rifle with a bronze plaque inscribed by their interior minister. I did not feel happy about such things but I was a loyal servant of the state myself. I had to obey orders too, orders given to me by Mr. Andropov. To refuse the chairman of the KGB would have been suicide for me."

Later, as a result of this interview, which he gave to a British newspaper, Kalugin was arrested by Scotland Yard and held for 24 hours while the Director of Public Prosecutions pondered his case. He decided that there was not enough evidence to proceed on a charge of conspiracy to commit murder. After his brush with British justice Kalugin said: "My participation in his death was precisely zero."

THE MYSTERY ASSASSIN

As to the assassin and the poisoned umbrella – they have vanished into history along with the regime that made them. Books since published in post-communist Sofia suggest that the assassin may be a retired Bulgarian diplomat living in his nation's capital, but Markov's friends dismiss this. Scotland Yard enquiries in his country as well as exhaustive checks in Britain after the attack have failed to turn up a culprit.

The death of Markov has gone unavenged long after the dictator who ordered his demise has himself fallen. The file on his death disappeared from Bulgarian secret service offices just after the collapse of the regime in 1990 and there is little hope now of anyone being brought to book for the murder.

His widow Annabella took some solace from a visit to Bulgaria after the fall of communism when she stood in a crowd of 100,000 people in freezing temperatures and heard them reel off the names of those murdered under Zhivkov's regime – with

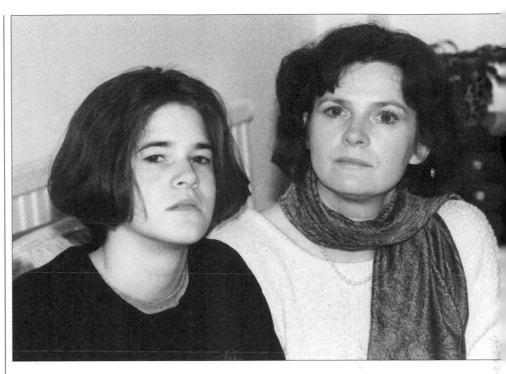

the cry of "killer!" to Zhivkov after every name. When it came to the name of Georgi Markov there was the biggest cheer of them all. He was loved by the Bulgarian people because he managed to make them laugh at their rulers – and there is nothing that a dictator fears quite so much as being laughed at; it means he is no longer feared.

But perhaps there is one epitaph to his memory that the writer – a humanitarian figure who believed in the ultimate good of man – would be pleased with. Early tests of a "magic bullet" treatment for cancer, based on the poison used to kill him, have shown remarkable results. Professor Philip Thorpe of the University of Texas South West Medical Centre says the first trials on patients have been "uncommonly good".

The therapy uses a monoclonal antibody linked to ricin. The ricin antibody recognises molecules exclusive to a certain type of blood cell. Once it finds them it sticks and delivers the fatal ricin to the cell. Fifteen patients with a cancer called B-Cell lymphoma, or non-Hodgkin's lymphoma, which causes more than 3,000 deaths each year in Britain, took part in the trial in 1993. Professor Thorpe reported that six of them had the size of their tumour reduced by more than half within a week of therapy.

If nothing else came from his death, Markov would surely smile at such lifesaving progress coming from the very venom that killed him.

Above: *A grown-up Sasha, Markov's daughter, poses with her widowed mother in London in 1991, two years after the hated communist regime that killed a loving husband and father had been consigned to the scrapheap of history.*

THE ASSASSIN AND THE POISONED UMBRELLA HAVE VANISHED INTO HISTORY ALONG WITH THE REGIME THAT MADE THEM

WHEN IT CAME TO THE NAME OF MARKOV THERE WAS THE BIGGEST CHEER OF ALL. HE WAS LOVED BY THE BULGARIAN PEOPLE

JOHN LIST
The Murderous Dad

It was a horrific case but, at the same time, it should have been an easy one for the police to solve. A family had been wiped out except for the father, who automatically became the chief suspect. Yet it was to be two decades before the forces of law and order caught up with killer and arch-hypocrite John List.

John Emil List was a modest man with much to be modest about. He looked like the humdrum, churchgoing accountant that he was. He neither smoked nor drank, had no interest in women or gambling and rarely took a vacation. He was parsimonious to the nth degree – turning the heat in the family's rambling mansion home so low in winter that all were forced to wear boiler suits to stay warm. German was the language spoken in the home in New Jersey, even though the furthest List had gotten to the land of his forefathers was a brochure from a travel agency. It was a miserable life for his wife Helen, their three children and his elderly mother – made more miserable by his dire financial straits and insistence on Bible-bashing at every given opportunity.

List, a man troubled by demons we can only guess at, decided to end what he saw as his family's "suffering" in this world. On a cold, foggy night in November 1971 – plagued by his children's apparent ungodliness, distraught at the looming spectre of financial ruin clouding his ordered life – John List took two handguns and wiped out his wife, three children and mother. The Friday before the massacre his daughter Patricia, 16, had told her high school drama teacher in the bucolic town of Westfield, New Jersey, that she was afraid her father was going to kill her – acting, in his eyes, was akin to prostitution. The teacher thought her prophesy nothing more than teenaged histrionics although she had told him: "He called us around the table and said he would have to kill us because he could no longer support us. He said he could not look after us the way he wanted to."

Her drama teacher never acted on her pleas and on Tuesday, November 9 1971, John List set about his macabre plan. He cancelled newspaper, milk and mail deliveries, informed the schools his children attended that the family would be visiting a sick relative out of town and told his bosses at a local bank that he was taking the day off sick.

LIST, A MAN TROUBLED BY DEMONS WE CAN ONLY GUESS AT, DECIDED TO END WHAT HE SAW AS HIS FAMILY'S "SUFFERING"

Opposite: *The seemingly timid John List murdered his family.*

Below: *John List after a brilliant piece of forensic modelling had led to his capture.*

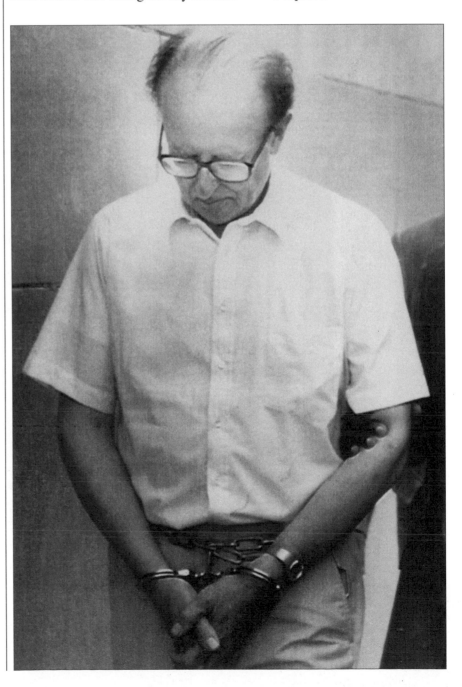

Behind the locked doors of the rambling, run-down mansion that was the unhappy family home, List executed his loved ones one by one. It was not until a month later, the house still brightly lit, that police broke into 431 Hillside Avenue with Edward Illiano, the drama teacher who had heard Patricia's fears first hand. Inside they saw a vision of hell. Laid out on the floor of the mansion's old ballroom were Helen List, aged 46, next to children John Frederick, 15, Frederick Michael, 13, and Patricia. John's body alone was riddled with ten bullets, although autopsies showed that death was brought about for all of them with a single bullet in the back of the head.

List's 84-year-old mother Alma was found on the third floor underneath a sloping roof near a bathub. List had attemped to drag her body downstairs but was unable to do so. Police found a filing cabinet in the house with the murder weapons along with five letters – one to his employer, one to his wife's mother, one to his mother's sister, one to his wife's sister and one to his local pastor – a rambling five page self-justification in which List tried to explain what led him to such a gruesome act. He wrote: "I know that what has been done is wrong from all that I have been taught and that any reasons I might give will not make it right. But you will at least possibly understand why I felt I had to do this."

DESPERATE TIMES

"I wasn't earning anywhere near enough to support us. Everything I tried seemed to fall to pieces. True, we could have gone bankrupt and maybe gone on welfare. But… knowing the type of location that one would have to live in, plus the environment for the children, plus the effect on them knowing they were on welfare was just more than I thought they could or should endure…

"With Pat being so determined to get into acting I was also fearful about what that might do to her continuing to be a Christian. Also with Helen, not going to

---

DEATH WAS BROUGHT ABOUT FOR ALL OF LIST'S FAMILY WITH A SINGLE BULLET IN THE BACK OF THE HEAD

Below: *John List pictured with the family he massacred. Daughter Patricia stands behind, next to him is his wife Helen and sons John and Frederick.*

church. The whole family seems to be slipping from Christianity. I knew this would harm the family eventually. At least I am certain all have gone to heaven now. If this had gone on who knows if this would be the case. I am sure many will say 'How could anyone do such a horrible thing?' My only answer is it isn't easy…

"It may seem cowardly to have always shot from behind but I didn't want any of them to know even at the last second that I had to do this… I am only concerned with making my peace with God and of this I am assured because of Christ dying even for me. P.S. Mother is in the hallway in the attic, 3rd floor. She was too heavy to move." He also said he had got down on his hands and knees and prayed after every killing – comfort for his soul that did little good for his innocent victims.

A QUICK GETAWAY

John Emil List, however, had vanished by the time police trawled trough the scene of indescribable horror. List, 46, left behind everything that identified him – his wallet, his driver's licence, his college class ring, even his overcoat and boots. He had methodically wiped up the blood from the executions with a towel – and eerily left classical music playing on an intercom system that stretched throughout the rambling 19-room mansion – before vanishing into the great expanse of North America. His first trip was to a bank where he withdrew $2,100 in bonds belonging to his mother. Then he drove to New York's Kennedy Airport where his Chevy car was found by authorities two days after the discovery of the bodies on December 7. James Moran, the Westfield Police Chief who was among the first of the lawmen to witness the rotting bodies in that room, made a vow to himself to track List down until the day he died. In the end he didn't succeed – but he did nevertheless live to see justice done.

For the next 18 years John List lived as a phantom in America. James Moran knew he was alive, knew he had adopted a new identity somewhere, but every lead drew a blank. In the first days and weeks after the discovery of the bodies the publicity was intense; America, brutalised as it is by violent crime, was sickened to its core by a man capable of such a monstrous act.

Tip-off lines to the FBI and police burned with information – policemen logged thousands of man hours following up leads that proved to be false. The insignificant List, who served as a private in World War Two and a reservist in the Korean War, had vanished off the face of the earth.

In Westfield in the weeks following the murder the List house became a kind of gruesome tourist attraction with people driving by to stare at the turn-of-the-century structure. Local children nicknamed it the "Norman Bates Motel" after the grisly murder site in the Hitchcock thriller *Psycho*. The attraction lasted little more than a year – it was mysteriously destroyed by fire in 1972. By then, a full 12 months after the killings, the trail had gone colder than an Arctic night. While frustrated FBI agents trawled across America, South America and Europe, John Emil List was living in a small town near Denver, Colorado. And for his new life he had taken out a new name – Robert P. Clark. The insignificant accountant with an obsession for orderliness and religion was working at his profession and attending the same kind of Lutheran church that he had left behind in New Jersey.

Above: *Robert Clark, otherwise known as John List, arrives at court to answer for his savage murders.*

HE SAID HE HAD GOT DOWN ON HIS HANDS AND KNEES AND PRAYED AFTER EVERY KILLING – COMFORT FOR HIS SOUL

On November 22 1971, 12 days after the killings, he had applied for a new Social Security number – in America the key to a new identity. Anyone under 50 can get a number without question and his was taken out in the name of Robert Peter Clark, residing at Motel Deville, 650 W. Paltax St., Denver, Colorado.

On the application he listed his parents as dead and his year of birth as being 1931. He did what so many on the run from justice failed to do – camouflaged himself by hiding in plain sight. His first job was as a night cook in a roadside diner, but he soon plucked up enough courage to list himself in the phone book as an accountant. He was back at his old trade… and he had managed to get away with murder.

Above: **FBI posters cry out for information on List.**
Below: **Finally List is caught.**

In 1977, so confident of life in his new identity, he courted a divorcee called Delores Miller whom he had met through a church singles group. Delores had many of the qualities of his murdered wife – before she strayed from the path of righteousness – and soon they were a couple in all but marriage. He put that right in 1985 when she became the second Mrs. List – and, in many respects, the sixth victim of the unfeeling monster.

A WILD GOOSE CHASE

Throughout these years the hunt continued for him without success. The only things that brought it into the public mind were occasional newspaper articles about the murders on anniversary dates. "Police Still Pursue Mass Killer", "14 Years And No List", "Police Still Baffled", they screamed with monotonous regularity. List lived a life of monotony and regularity, scrupulously avoiding any trouble, anything that might lay a trail to his new life in a new town 2,000 miles from the murders. Chief Moran laboured ceaselessly, checking out the leads and calls that flooded in each time a newspaper resurrected the murders, but each time there was no luck. Moran, however, remained optimistic, saying: "So he was careful, so he was keeping a low profile. So he was a nondescript kind of guy, so he never did one single thing to draw attention to himself. Nonetheless, I knew that one day he would make a mistake and that someone would be waiting to snap the cuffs on him. I hoped so much it would be me."

In the latter half of the 1980s List moved with his wife to Richmond, Virginia – now less than 500 miles from the murder scene. Still wimpy, still churchgoing, he nevertheless enjoyed watching TV on a regular basis and one of his favourite programme was *America's Most Wanted*, a weekly expose of the killers, conmen, rapists, robbers and bad guys who were wanted by the FBI. It was the programme that would eventually lead to his capture.

America's Most Wanted was approached by an officer on the murder squad and

asked if it could broadcast an appeal about List. Margaret Roberts, the show's managing editor, was keen to help, but hampered by the lack of recent photos of him. Michael Lindner, an executive producer of the show which had an impressive track record of catching fugitives, thought he could solve the problem with the aid of a 47-year-old commercial photographer and forensic sculptor called Frank Bender. Bender had specialised in recent years in creating busts of fugitives for law enforcement authorities across America. In the case of List, all he had to work with was a 1971 photo, a computerised update on his image and a police description. "It was a challenge," said Bender, adding: "But I think I had worked on harder projects."

Bender's journey into forensic sculpture had begun in 1977 by accident. Accompanying a friend on a tour of the

THE FORENSIC SCULPTOR TACKED UP ENLARGED PHOTOS OF LIST IN THE KITCHEN OF HIS HOME AND STUDIED THEM INTENSELY

Left: *Commercial photographer and forensic sculptor Frank Bender specialised in creating busts of fugitives for law enforcement authorities across America.*

Below: *All Bender had to work on to create the bust of List was a 1971 photo, a computerised update on his image and a police description. "It was a challenge," said Bender. "But I think I had worked on harder projects."*

Philadelphia morgue he had been shown the corpse of a woman shot three times through the head at point-blank range. Because of wounds and advanced decomposition, identification of the body was impossible. As an artistic experiment he rebuilt her face – and the woman was identified two days after he completed the cast in clay. Since then his work as a "physiognomic reconstructionist" had continued unabated and he was regarded as the foremost expert in the field.

A PSYCHOLOGICAL PROFILE

Bender turned to a friend, criminal psychologist Richard Walter from Michigan, for help in fleshing out details about List and what made him tick. Walter speculated that he would be the kind of guy who wouldn't be a health freak, that he was a worrier whose age would show. He would probably wear the same kind of eyeglasses, show the same nervous strain in his face, that his hair would have receded further, leaving a very high forehead and a partially bald cranium. He would have sagging jowls and a downturned, saddened look. Bender was convinced the psychological profile was right and set to work making the clay bust of the fugitive.

Day after day he moulded the face. He tacked up enlarged photos of List in the kitchen of his home and studied them intensely. He glued rubber erases to a fibreglass skull to attain the right thickness and then filled in the gaps with the clay. He kept reminding himself of what Walter had

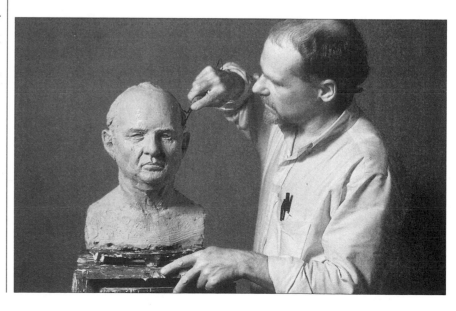

Above: *On May 1 1990, John List was sentenced to life imprisonment without the possibility of parole.*

"HIS ACTS STAND AS A PERMANENT, PATHETIC AND PROFANE EXAMPLE OF MAN'S INHUMANITY TO MAN"

said about him ageing, about how he would look aged 63 and not 46. Finally, satisfied with what he saw, he made a plaster mould that he then filled in with fibreglass. Afterwards he painted the model with flesh tones and handed it over to the producers of *America's Most Wanted*.

On Sunday May 21 1989 the show aired... and luck was on the side of justice. Robert Clark, nee John List, had travelled to a church social and so missed his favourite show, one that chronicled in depth his crimes, culminating with the sculpture and description of him as a pen-pusher, quiet, a nonentity. Afterwards there were 300 phone calls within minutes, all from people who claimed to know the wherabouts and new identity of John List. But only one of them proved to be correct and that came from Wanda Flannery, a friend of his wife Dolores back in Denver. "That's Bob!" she screamed when the image of the bust played on her TV screen. She rang the hotline and gave the operator the name, address and phone number of Bob Clark in Virginia.

Tracing down the hundreds of leads took time, but on June 1 1989, at 10.00 am, FBI agent Kevin August from Richmond, together with three colleagues, knocked at the door of the Clark home in Midlothian, near Richmond. Delores answered the door and mumbled the address of the small-town law firm where her husband was working. There, a little over one hour later, August confronted the fugitive and asked him: "Are you John List?" "No I am not," he lied, but August was convinced.

Three agents pinned him to the wall while August read him his rights. "My name is Robert Clark," said List, trying to bluff it out. But two hours later a fingerprint test proved him to be John List – fingerprints on file at the police station where he had applied for a firearms permit for the weapons to slaughter his family. The game was up after 18 years.

Former police chief Moran was one of the first to hear the news. "It's him?" was his first reaction, stunned that he had been caught by a clever model of his features when every method of modern detection had failed to find him in close to two decades of searching. "Then I said it was the best thing that had ever happened to me. That bum should never get away with what he did." List was charged with five counts of murder and caged pending a trial – the outcome of which was a foregone conclusion, even though at his arraignment on July 10 he pleaded not guilty, and insisted he was Robert Clark, not John Emil List.

A SENSIBLE PLEA

In February 1990 his attorney made him see sense and admit to being the fugitive, yet he pleaded not guilty to first degree murder at his full trial in April, claiming he had acted out of love for his family and that it was not a premeditated massacre. Clearly, with the letters left behind and his escape route planned, this was a nonsense. List's confessions to a psychiatrist were read out which showed him to be the ultimate, sneering criminal who believed himself above both God's law and that of man. In the end the jury, nine days after the trial began, found him guilty of all five counts of wilful murder. John List had been brought to book by a lump of clay fashioned by the skilful hands of a man who had never ever seen him.

When he was sentenced on May 1 1990 to life imprisonment without the possibility of parole, John List told the court: "I wish to inform the court that I remain truly sorry for the tragedy which happened in 1971. I feel that due to my mental state at the time I was unaccountable for what happened. I ask all those who were affected by this for their forgiveness, their understanding and their prayers. Thank You."

Judge Wertheimer lashed him from the bench: "His acts stand as a permanent, pathetic and profane example to the potential of man's inhumanity to man. They will not be soon or easily forgotten, and the name of John Emil List will be eternally synonymous with the concepts of selfishness, horror and evil."

John List rots in jail – and finally his family can rest in peace.